LIVING HOPE

The Future and Christian Faith

David H. Jensen

WESTMINSTER JOHN KNOX PRESS
LOUISVILLE · KENTUCKY

For John and Gretchen Jensen

© 2010 David H. Jensen

First edition
Published by Westminster John Knox Press
Louisville, Kentucky

10 11 12 13 14 15 16 17 18 19—10 9 8 7 6 5 4 3 2 1

Scripture quotations from the New Revised Standard Version of the Bible are copy-right © 1989 by the Division of Christian Education of the National Council of the Churches of Christ in the U.S.A. and are used by permission.

Excerpts from the *Book of Confessions* are reprinted with the permission of the Office of the General Assembly, Presbyterian Church (U.S.A.).

Book design by Sharon Adams
Cover design by Eric Walljasper, Minneapolis, MN

Library of Congress Cataloging-in-Publication Data

Jensen, David Hadley
    Living hope : the future and christian faith / David H. Jensen. — 1st ed.
        p. cm.
    Includes bibliographical references.
    ISBN 978-0-664-23314-3 (alk. paper)
    1. Eschatology. 2. Hope—Religious aspects—Christianity. I. Title.

BT821.3.J46 2010
236—dc22
                                                                        2010017886

Most Westminster John Knox Press books are available at special quantity discounts when purchased in bulk by corporations, organizations, and special-interest groups. For more information, please e-mail SpecialSales@wjkbooks.com.

Contents

Introduction

Christians are people who hope. We are not, of course, the only people who hope. Yet Christians hope in distinctive ways, and our hopes are sometimes different from other visions of hope that present themselves in the world. This book introduces Christian *eschatology*, a word that means the "study of the last things." From the earliest days of the church, Christians have looked toward the future. Those who followed Jesus were convinced that he was beginning something new, something that would be fulfilled at a future point in history when God's fullness would extend throughout the earth. In the midst of internal struggle and external persecution, those early Christians did not give up on hope. As they looked toward the future and God's coming reign of justice and peace, the early Christians also understood their hope for the future to be grounded in the good news that Jesus Christ, God's Son, had already come and was present wherever two or three believers gathered in his name. If the early church longed for the future, it did not forget the past or neglect the present. For this reason, Christian eschatology is never only about the future or about the "last things." Rather, it connects these "last things" to the new things that God has already done and is doing in Jesus Christ. Christian hope, therefore, does not simply look forward but glances backward as well, all the while keeping our feet firmly planted in the present.

This book offers an introduction to eschatology. I have written it without technical language and with minimal notes. Though people with significant theological training might find it interesting, I have designed it primarily for beginning seminary and college students and for persons in the Christian churches without formal theological education. Over the course of my teaching at a Presbyterian seminary and in adult education settings in many churches, I have become convinced that there are few topics that befuddle Christians as much as eschatology. Words like "Armageddon," the "Second Coming" and the "Last Judgment" strike fear in some hearts and disbelief in others. Most of the churches where I have taught and most of the students that I currently teach might be described as "mainline Protestant." They are varied in their cultural, political, and economic backgrounds, but most share one thing in common: they tend to talk little about the "last things." They talk little not because they think topics such as the resurrection of the dead and return of Christ are unimportant but because they're often unsure how to address them. In this sense, they're different from other, mostly fundamentalist North American Christians who speak profusely and confidently about Christ's return, the Last Judgment, and the antichrist. For fundamentalists, the "last things" are not greeted with silence but stand at the center of faith: they depict the urgency of evangelism and the life-and-death consequences of faith.

I write this book for Christians—Protestant and Catholic—who are confused by their churches' avoidance of eschatology, but who are at the same time troubled by fundamentalists' glib talk about the end of days. I write it with a two-pronged guiding question: What do Christians believe about the future as it comes in Jesus Christ, and what implications does that belief have for daily living?

I write, moreover, as a Reformed theologian. I am a member of a Presbyterian church, teach at a Presbyterian seminary, and lead adult education classes most often at Presbyterian churches. As a Presbyterian, I stand within the branch of Protestantism often dubbed the "Reformed tradition." My conversation partners in this book, therefore, are typically Reformed: I engage the Bible primarily and secondarily I draw from John Calvin's *Institutes* (ed. John T. McNeill, trans. Ford Lewis Battles, LCC [Philadelphia: Westminster Press, 1960]) and the historic confessions of that Reformed heritage. When I cite Scripture, I use the NRSV; when I cite Reformed confessions, I use numerical notation from the *Book of Confessions* (Louisville, KY: Office of the General Assembly, Presbyterian Church (U.S.A.), 1996). Yet my conversation partners move far beyond these resources: I also engage a wide range of resources from the history of the church—ancient, medieval, and modern—as well as voices that are not explicitly theological.

The book contains four parts. The first surveys some of the varied biblical themes as they address hope, God's future, and the end of days. The second, which forms the heart of the book, focuses on some guiding themes of Christian hope. Here I trace the foundations of a Christian anticipation of the future that is grounded in the past and attentive to the present. Chapters in this section outline Jesus' proclamation of the kingdom of God, the resurrection of the body, Christ's promised return, the Last Judgment, and the new creation. Part 3 turns to more controversial and disputed themes, themes that are perhaps more prominent among fundamentalists than among those for whom I write this book. Here I address several misunderstandings of Christian hope as they relate to the so-called "rapture," heaven and hell, the millennium and Armageddon, and the antichrist. Attention to the themes outlined in part 2 helps Christians to address some of the controversy surrounding themes in part 3. Finally, the book turns in part 4 to some concrete ways Christians embody hope in their daily living. Thus, I conclude with baptism, the Lord's Supper, and our labors for justice and peace as practices permeated by hope.

Like my other writing projects, this piece has been cobbled together over time, in the midst of trial and joy. I have many to thank for whatever wisdom is in it, though the mistakes are my own. Colleagues at Austin Presbyterian Theological Seminary continue to make professional life collegial. Friends in the Workgroup for Constructive Theology stimulate my own writing every spring. Donald McKim encouraged me to write this book during several conversations. He and the editorial staff at Westminster John Knox Press continue to be advocates of my work. Students in my course in eschatology and Christian hope have been invaluable as this project came together over several years. Members of First Presbyterian Church, Georgetown, Texas, and First Presbyterian Church, Destin, Florida, offered many questions and delightful conversation during retreat and Sunday school sessions. The 2009 meeting of the Association of Presbyterian Church Educators provided lively exchanges on all things eschatological. My family—Molly, Grace, and Finn—continues to show me living faces of hope in the everyday. I dedicate this book to my parents, John and Gretchen, who taught me to hope and refuse to give up hope during Dad's ongoing struggle with cancer.

PART 1

Biblical Perspectives

Many Christians approach the Bible in the life of faith as a book of *answers*, as a text that offers a uniform perspective on questions of life and death. The phrase ". . . the Bible tells me so" suggests as much. So, too, does another quip: "The Bible says it; I believe it." Yet the witness of the Christian Scriptures is far richer and more complex than either of these phrases suggests. The biblical text says not one thing over and over but multiple things in varied and diverse voices. This section of the book explores some of the depth and variety of the biblical traditions as they bear witness to Christian hope.

1

The Bible Tells Me So?
Scripture and Christian Hope

"The world's going to end within our lifetimes; I'm convinced of it," Demetrius said to his companions. It was fellowship time at First Presbyterian Church, that important window of time on Sunday between the education hour and worship. Typically, the conversations over coffee and donuts at this gathering were more lighthearted, focused on friendships and families, the latest events in town, or even that afternoon's football games. But today, the standard fluff of small talk didn't seem appropriate. Most of those gathered around the tables had just heard a presentation on global warming in the contemporary-issues adult education class. One member of the congregation, a faculty member of the local college who teaches environmental studies, presented data on climate change, complete with satellite photographs showing the melting polar ice caps and deforestation of large swaths of rain forests. During the hour, people in this class heard that eight of the hottest ten years on record have occurred during the last decade, that habitats for countless species worldwide are slowly (and sometimes rapidly) disappearing, and that all evidence seems to point to our increasing appetite for fossil fuels. It was late October, but it felt like summer, with temperatures outside set to break another record. The caffeine and sugar supplied in the fellowship hall only seemed to fuel the agitation of those gathered.

"Yes," Demetrius continued, "the world's surely going to end soon. God's just fed up with all the mess we've made of the planet, and we sit here under judgment. Our only hope is for God to heal the damage we've done. Isn't that a Christian belief? That sin makes the world a rotten place, deserving of God's judgment? Isn't that what our hope points to? God setting things right again? That's what I hope for: God making all things new."

"Now hang on a minute, Demetrius; you're getting way ahead of yourself," chimed in Sarah. "I won't argue with you that things are terrible, and we don't need to look only at climate change to tell us that. I know that things are bad as soon as I wake up each morning. Have you been reading about the sorry state of our public schools? The metal detectors, the drugs, the violence, and they don't end when the school bell rings. When our children go home, they watch people killing each another on TV. Good Lord, things are bad, and most of it is because of the violence that spreads like wildfire in our society. But that's no proof that the world's going to end soon. As a Christian, I don't think much about the end times. I know that sometime the world will end, but I'm pretty sure that I won't be around for it. The world's been around a pretty long time, and my lifetime is just a blip on the screen. I don't think God wants us to pay too much attention to the end of things; I think he wants us to make a difference now. Didn't Jesus' ministry focus on *this* world? Didn't Jesus say that he came so that we might have life and have it abundantly? The good life shouldn't be postponed until heaven; the good life is right here, right now, as we hope for the renewal of all things even in the midst of sin. Isn't that what the Bible teaches?"

"Oh, good grief!" lamented Carlos. "Weren't any of you listening to the presentation? You both are talking about hope and the end of the world like it was focused on us. While we stand here and argue, we are destroying the habitats of polar bears and penguins. Shouldn't we turn our attention to them and to the places that are suffering in the world? It's not about you; it's not about me; it's not about us; it's about God's world. When I read the Bible, I realize that I'm not at the center of the story; what I read is a story between God and creation. We can't predict the end of the world, Demetrius, but we can care for others. The Bible tells me that."

"I think each one of you is too hopeful," sighed Martha. "The Bible tells me that sin has always been around and will always be around as long as there are people. All this talk about what we hope for seems like a waste of time. I don't so much hope for a brave new world as much as I resign myself to the reality of sin in that world. We shouldn't hold out much hope for our own efforts to change things. All the grand experiments that human beings have tried wind up failing in the end. I don't place hope in anything that human beings do. 'Vanity of vanities, all is vanity'; isn't that what it says in Ecclesiastes? There will be no end to the mess. It'll always be around. The Bible tells me that, and it's confirmed each day of my life when I walk out the door. God is my only hope."

Martha's comment spurs the others to argue their points. Each person seems to have evidence from the Bible to support his or her own line of argument, and in the ensuing conversation, each becomes more convinced of his or her position. As they argue, however, time marches on, and soon they notice everyone else heading toward the sanctuary. Time has expired for this conversation, perhaps to be resumed next Sunday, perhaps to be forgotten in the hype of next Sunday's football game. But for a while at least, it held their attention and was certainly the first time that any of those gathered had talked about "the end of the world" with such tenacity.

What does the Bible teach us about the "end times"? What does it say about the purpose of our lives and the life of the planet? What does the Bible teach us about hope? What voices, in the conversation that we have just heard, also find resonance in the pages of Christian Scripture as we read and interpret them together?

MANY VOICES

Determining what the Bible "says" about a particular topic is notoriously tricky business. Because the numerous books that compose the Christian Scriptures have been gathered together over several centuries, written and edited by countless hands, many voices rather than one voice are represented within them. Take, for example, the voices of Paul and James. In Romans, Paul writes, "For we hold that a person is justified by faith apart from works prescribed by the law" (Rom. 3:28), verses that have nourished Protestants in their piety, teaching them to trust faith and not their own deeds. But in James we also read that "faith by itself, if it has no works, is dead" (Jas. 2:17), verses that have proved vexing to Christians who hold a "faith alone" perspective on piety. These are voices that cannot be conflated. They sound different because they *are* different. Christian faith gets diluted, moreover, if we think that we need to choose Paul over James or James over Paul. Each voice says indispensable things about faith and life, without which faith is immeasurably poorer. This is the case with nearly every subject of faith: salvation, Christ, God, church. The Bible says not one thing in one voice but many things in multiple voices. It stages not a solo but a chorus of witnesses.

The Bible says *many* things about the purpose, end, and promise of creation. In some sections, the Bible seems to point to an end of all things that is coming very soon. Demetrius represents a Christian who is struggling to come to grips with this message. But his is not the only voice. Other narratives of Scripture focus more on hope in the transformation of this life than in things yet to come. Sarah and Carlos are wrestling with these biblical voices. Finally, other strands of Scripture warn us against too much hope, reminding us of the abiding reality of sin and the naïveté of an optimistic notion of progress. Martha, in the previous conversation, is trying to make sense of those voices in the chorus of biblical witnesses. The Bible has diverse views of the future, each arising in its own context, each addressing different facets of God's promises to creation. Each of the three perspectives—an imminent end focused on the future, a delayed end that turns our attention to the present, and a more chastened view of hope that warns us against optimism—is present in Scripture. Each informs our reading of the others. None of them, moreover, captures the sum of Christian hope. Let's look at each of these voices in greater detail.

THE PROPHETS: THIS-WORLDLY HOPE

The prophets of ancient Israel call people to account when they fall short of the covenant God establishes with them. When Israel ignores the plight of the poor, the orphan, the resident alien, and the widow, the prophets utter divine judgment. When the people wander after foreign gods, the prophets call the people back to worship of the one true God. The prophets document God's abiding faithfulness to Israel despite the multiple ways it stumbles in maintaining covenant, and they often utter judgment and hope in the same breath. Amos, for example, says, "I hate, I despise your festivals, and I take no delight in your solemn assemblies" and "Let justice roll down like waters, and righteousness like an ever-flowing stream" (Amos 5:21, 24). In judging Israel's false piety, Amos also hopes for God's transformation of the world, where all will partake in the fullness of life and God's justice. These hopes are not for the next life; they are for the future of this people and this world.

Most of the prophets do not pin hopes to a life beyond the grave. Even in Ezekiel, whose vision of the valley of dry bones (Ezek. 37:1–14) is sometimes cited as an analog to resurrection, explicit hope for the afterlife is absent. Some of the prophets, including Ezekiel, mention Sheol, or the realm of the dead. But Sheol is neither a place of damnation or salvation in any sense that Christians have become accustomed to believing. Rather Sheol represents the inescapability of death (Ezek. 31:14–17) in every life.

Hope, for the prophets, is rooted in God's faithfulness to the people Israel, the calling of a people home to the new city of Zion. Yet hope does not end with the covenant people. When God renews the covenant with Israel the world also finds a home there. Isaiah records this hope: "Nations shall come to your light, and kings to the brightness of your dawn" (Isa. 60:3), where even Gentiles may serve as priests (66:20–21). Growing ever wider, the circle of hope in the Prophets eventually encompasses all who seek the Lord. Focused on this world, this hope knows no national boundaries.

REALISTIC HOPE: WISDOM LITERATURE

The Bible doesn't always present future hope as a virtue. Wisdom literature steers our attention away from the future and toward the present, warning against vanity, pride, and our abiding temptation to attribute much to ourselves: "For the fate of humans and the fate of animals is the same; as one dies, so dies the other. They all have the same breath, and humans have no advantage over the animals; for all is vanity. All go to one place; all are from the dust, and all turn to dust again" (Eccl. 3:19–20). The hope of human life, for Ecclesiastes, is not its superiority to the rest of creation nor the mark that human beings make upon history; neither is it in eternal life. Rather, hope lies in the ordinary matters of this life: work, relationships, food, and conversation. Unrestrained speculation for what lies ahead is little more than a diversion from the lives we are called to live today. Hope for the future should not divert us from ordinary things we often take for granted. As all is destined for dust, we ought to enjoy our fellow travelers and the journey along our way.

APOCALYPTIC HOPE

Other strands of the Old Testament frame hope in yet other ways. Some of the most recent books of the Hebrew Scriptures bear the traces of an apocalyptic hope influenced by Israel's time spent in exile in Babylon. What is apocalyptic hope? This strand of hope displays at least these four characteristics or beliefs: 1) despair over the world's present state of affairs; 2) the idea that the world is in the hands of evil powers, headed toward imminent destruction; 3) the belief that God will intervene on behalf of the righteous, triumph over evil, and bring about a new paradise; and 4) the belief that we can see signs of this imminent intervention in present events.

Daniel is the chief example of this strand of hope in the Old Testament, a book saturated with visions, promising the ultimate victory of Israel against those who would vanquish it and eternal life for the righteous. In Daniel's visions, heavenly powers defeat terrestrial powers that enslave others: a cosmic battle of good and evil unfolds, with good triumphing in the end. The collective hope of the people awaits Israel at the end of days, where divine power manifests itself in fullness (Dan. 11). But Daniel also records strands of individual hope, offering a vision of resurrection: "'Many of those who sleep in the dust of the earth shall awake, some to everlasting life, and some to shame and everlasting contempt. Those who are wise shall shine like the brightness of the sky, and those who lead many to righteousness, like the stars forever and ever'" (12:2–3). Amid the tumult of the present day, Israel abides in a God who intervenes on behalf of God's people, restoring hope to that people, promising the final defeat of their enemies, offering the promise of eternal life for those who are faithful and everlasting contempt to those who are not. In Daniel, divine justice has eternal consequences.

JESUS: APOCALYPTIC PROPHET?

Interpreting Jesus in relation to these three strands of hope—this-worldly, realistic, and apocalyptic—is difficult. Depending on the Gospel one reads, Jesus offers different words on the end of the world and what we hope for. Mark, the earliest Gospel, sounds the most apocalyptic. In Mark, Jesus warns of kingdom rising against kingdom, earthquakes, and famine that are "'but the beginning of the birth pangs'" (Mark 13:8). Central to this apocalypse is the Son of Man, who will come in clouds of power and glory: "'Then he will send out the angels, and gather his elect from the four winds, from the ends of the earth to the ends of heaven'" (13:27). Earlier in Mark, Jesus identifies himself with the Son of Man, in three foretellings of his death and resurrection (Mark 8:31–38; 9:30–32; 10:32–34), and he echoes this identification later in his defense before the council (14:62). From start to finish, Mark's Jesus announces the end of the age, inviting those who would follow him to turn away from the present order in repentance. Jesus comes as hope for the world, heralding a new age, in which Israel renews its covenant and in which strangers to that covenant are welcomed. Jesus is the Jewish prophet whose death and resurrection are also lights unto the Gentiles. At his death, a centurion recognizes him as God's Son; upon his resurrection, he goes ahead of his followers to Galilee, at the threshold of the Gentile world. If Jesus is an apocalyptic prophet, he is not an otherworldly prophet, for his ministry is decidedly this-worldly, offering hope to the world in healing from disease, repenting sins, and restoring the lost to table fellowship.

Luke's Gospel expresses the relationship between apocalypse and this-worldly liberation most clearly. In the Magnificat, the coming of Mary's son dethrones the powerful and uplifts the lowly, filling the hungry with good things and sending the rich away empty (Luke 1:52–53) and expressing hope that salvation is not postponed until the next world. Yet at the end of his earthly ministry, Jesus' last words also express hope for life beyond death, extended to a consummate outsider, the criminal hanging on the cross next to Jesus. "'Jesus,'" this man asks, "'remember me when you come into your kingdom.'" To which Jesus replies, "'Truly I tell you, today you will be with me in Paradise'" (Luke 23:42–43). The One who promises liberation for the world also bears upon his lips the words of eternal life.

In John, Jesus' apocalypticism is more muted. Jesus also appears in John as the inaugurator of a new age, but he is shorn of any wild-eyed fervor. God's kingdom is not chiefly a future promise but a present reality witnessed in Jesus' person. All those who follow Jesus *already* participate in the new age. "'I came that they may have life, and have it abundantly,'" Jesus claims (John 10:10). John's Gospel expresses a *realized eschatology*, that the events of the "end times" are already present or realized in Jesus and in the new life he gives.

In the Gospels, Jesus embodies multiple strands of hope: he offers visions of an age yet to come but also promises that we can participate in that age in the present. He anticipates the coming of God's kingdom yet identifies that reign with himself. In his words are the promise of eternal life and the experience of that life right now. Jesus' hope is neither overly futuristic nor overly realized. If he is, as some would claim, an apocalyptic prophet, his proclamation of the end of the age does not linger in the distant future but summons the past and empowers the present.

REVELATION: CHRISTIAN APOCALYPSE

The Christian Scriptures, however, end on a decidedly apocalyptic note. If Jesus sounds apocalyptic now and then, Revelation is apocalyptic through and through. The last words of Scripture offer the grandest of all biblical visions: judgment of the wicked, defeat of the powerful, vindication of the righteous, and the renewal of heaven and earth. Revelation discerns ominous signs in the present age, personified in the Roman Empire, "'Babylon the great, mother of whores and of earth's abominations'" (Rev. 17:5). The power of Rome, epitomized in its emperors, makes war on Christ the Lamb, "'and the Lamb will conquer them, for he is Lord of lords and king of kings, and those with him are called and chosen and faithful'" (17:14). Though earth's powers seem to rage continually, their duration is evanescent in light of the One "who is and who was and who is to come" (1:4). If Revelation promises an imminent return of Christ, this return is not restricted to the future. The One who will come is also the one who *is*. Future hope, even in the most staggering of apocalypse, is sustained by Christ's continual presence, a hope not simply for people but for the entire creation: a new city, a new heaven, and a new earth (21:1–22:7). In the end, nothing that God creates will be left behind.

PETER AND PAUL: THE DELAY OF CHRIST'S IMMINENT RETURN

Paul, apostle to the Gentiles, expected the end of days to occur within his lifetime. The letter that scholars believe he wrote first, 1 Thessalonians, provides exhortation for Christian living in light of Christ's return. It also includes consolation for those who worry about people who have already died before Christ's return: "But we do not want you to be uninformed, brothers and sisters, about those who have died, so that you may not grieve as others do who have no hope. For since we believe that Jesus died and rose again, even so, through Jesus, God will bring with him those who have died" (1 Thess. 4:13–14). It is neither gain nor disadvantage to have died before Christ's return. Paul, moreover, expects to be alive when the Parousia—the final return of Christ—occurs: "Then we who are alive, who are left, will be caught up in the clouds together with them to meet the Lord in the air; and so we will be with the Lord forever" (4:17).

On this question, Paul was far from unique. Most of the first generation of Christians assumed an imminent return. But something happened along the way to the Parousia. Christ did not return in glory, at least in the way that Paul and others had anticipated. That first generation of Christians came face-to-face with what all generations of Christians have had to recognize ever since: the *delay* of Christ's return. By the time Paul writes the letter to the Romans, for example, language suggesting an imminent return is more muted. Paul portrays the death and resurrection of God's people not only as a future promise in light of Christ's return but also a present reality: "So you also must consider yourselves dead to sin and alive to God in Christ Jesus" (Rom. 6:11). Instead of understanding this delay as a disappointment, Paul focuses hope anew on Christ: the One whom Christians await has already come in the flesh, transforming our lives bound by sin into vessels of glory. As creation "waits with eager longing for the revealing of the children of God" (8:19), it is already being renewed moment by moment.

The Second Letter of Peter, which scholars generally hold to be the last biblical book to be composed, also expresses adjustment in the early church's anticipation of Christ's return:

> First of all you must understand this, that in the last days scoffers will come, scoffing and indulging their own lusts and saying, "Where is the promise of his coming? For ever since our ancestors died, all things continue as they were from the beginning of creation!" . . .
>
> But do not ignore this one fact, beloved, that with the Lord one day is like a thousand years, and a thousand years are like one day. (2 Pet. 3:3–4, 8)

The promise, rather than the time, of Christ's return is of the essence. The behavior of the saints who await the coming of the Lord does not simply prepare for Christ's coming but attests to his present transformation of the world.

JAMES: HOPEFUL REALISM?

The most difficult strand of Old Testament hope to locate within the New Testament is the hopeful realism of Wisdom literature. Because the writings that compose the New Testament were all written within less than a century—a time in which the expectation of Christ's imminent return was highly influential—there is less variety in the hope expressed in its pages. Yet within this context occurs the Letter of James, which warns against superfluous worry about tomorrow: "What is your life? For you are a mist that appears for a little while and then vanishes. Instead you ought to say, 'If the Lord wishes, we will live and do this or that'" (Jas. 4:14–15). Ecclesiastes hardly could have said it better. The hope that James stresses is not for an elusive future but for the present day, grounded by Christ's presence, focused on the most vulnerable in the midst: "Religion that is pure and undefiled before God, the Father, is this: to care for orphans and widows in their distress, and to keep oneself unstained by the world" (1:27). Christian hope, for James, has intensely this-worldly consequences and amounts to a pious diversion if it does not result in works of love for the poor and oppressed.

THE REALITY OF MANY VOICES

What does the Bible say about hope and about the last things? Scripture, as we have seen, says many things. If we recall the coffee-hour conversation that began this chapter, something in each of the perspectives appears within diverse biblical texts. Some biblical texts foresee an imminent end to the world as we know it through divine intervention; others focus hope squarely on this world, longing for God's establishment of justice and peace for all creation; still others warn against diversionary hopes that obscure the plight of the poor and the groaning of creation. Demetrius expects Christ to return very soon and finds ample witness of his perspective in Scripture. But Sarah and Carlos also read Scripture closely and urge Demetrius not to ignore the renewal in Christ that is present now by turning one's attention to the suffering world. Martha's voice is also present within Scripture, offering realism against hopes that cause us to ignore the present day. The church oversimplifies hope when it opts for one of these views to the exclusion of the others.

A hope that focuses only on an imminent return of the Lord, though it may be bolstered by reading apocalyptic biblical texts, winds up undermining the *present* transformation of the world by the grace of Jesus Christ. We cannot focus simply on Christ's return if we are not rooted in the good news of his life and ministry. The cosmic Son of Man also heals the sick, blesses children, and welcomes the stranger. His return only makes sense in light of these acts of healing that we encounter in his ministry and bear witness to today.

Yet we also blunt Christian faith if we focus only on the present. If there is no hope for the coming of a kingdom, if the present state of affairs is the final word, then faith degenerates into resignation. Fundamental to Christian faith is the knowledge that God is doing something new, drawing all into fuller life, and that this new thing cannot be reduced to the things that we do. While the participants in the conversation at the beginning of this chapter imply that each of their perspectives on Christian hope exclude the others, it might be more helpful to claim that they actually need one another to bear witness to Christian hope. Without Carlos and Sarah, Demetrius's voice becomes fatalistic futurism devoid of strength for the present; without Demetrius, Martha becomes resigned to the present state of affairs; without Martha and Demetrius, Carlos and Sarah wind up focusing on human actions to the exclusion of creation and God's activity in the world. The witness of Scripture is richer than no one voice can proclaim, especially in the arena of Christian hope.

QUESTIONS FOR DISCUSSION

1. Which voices in the Bible that speak of hope do you find most difficult to engage and understand? Which voices do you find most comforting and familiar? Why?
2. How do the books of the Bible, written centuries ago, continue to sustain hope today?

PART II

Guiding Themes of Christian Hope

What are the distinguishing characteristics of Christian hope? What makes Christian faith different from postures that place ultimate hope in people, places, and events other than God? What makes hope, in other words, Christian? The Bible, we have seen, offers many voices that give rise to hope. Amid these voices, however, emerge some prominent markers of hope. Christian hope points to the transformation of society in the kingdom of God, the victory over death witnessed in the resurrection, and the renewal of heaven and earth promised in the new creation. This section of the book examines each of these dimensions of hope as they bear on individual, social, and cosmic life.

2

The Kingdom of God

"Christian hope strikes me, in the end, as ultimately selfish," quipped Mark at the coffeehouse on University Avenue. He raised his hands for emphasis: "Come on, don't most Christians have a fairly simple view of faith: 'Believe this, believe that, and you, too, can have eternal life.' That's simple and that's it. Well, in my opinion, that's selfish. That means that Christians want to hold on to their lives so desperately that they will believe anything to sustain it. If that's what Christian faith boils down to, I want no part of it."

"I'm not sure if that's quite it," ventured Angela with hesitation. She knew that Mark, who had left a fundamentalist church three years ago, would be an interesting conversation partner. Angela had been struggling of late with some of the things she'd been hearing about Christian hope. It was the week after Easter Sunday, and she had heard much proclaimed in the sanctuary and then echoed in the voices of her extended family gathered for Easter dinner. It just didn't seem to make sense to her anymore. All this talk about hope beyond the grave. . . . What did it mean? Angela wasn't quite sure what she believed, and she was sure she couldn't proclaim it with the same confidence that she heard her pastor offer in the Easter sermon last Sunday. She had sought out Mark because she knew that he had struggled with some of these same questions. "But does Jesus talk a lot about eternal life?" she asked. "In all the Gospel stories that I remember, I hear him telling stories, welcoming strangers, healing the sick, proclaiming that people should confess their sin. Jesus turns our attention to others, not to ourselves, doesn't he?"

"Sure, Jesus says a lot of good things. His teachings I have no trouble with; it's mainly his fan club," argued Mark. Angela had seen that bumper sticker before in her neighborhood: "Jesus is all right; it's his fan club that annoys me."

"Christians are still basically selfish people," Mark continued. "And what's more, this business about saving one's soul, about eternal life, doesn't mesh at all with what we've learned from contemporary science. Listen to what physics and astronomy are saying to us: the human being isn't the center of the universe. The point of it all is not that we might have eternal life. We're one blip, one microsecond in the lifespan of the universe. We're not at the center of things; we're on the periphery, on a small planet hurtling through the galaxy, which is but one of billions of other galaxies."

"You have a point, Mark, but I still think you're making a large generalization about all Christians," said Angela. "Now, I'll grant that some would take a transactional or selfish view of faith: 'Believe this, and you will be rewarded.' But that's the very stuff that I hear Jesus arguing against in the Gospels. Jesus puts us in the midst of a much wider world. I think a lot of Christians are missing the point, but I'm not ready to give up on the fan club, not quite yet."

"But you've just named it, Angela," interrupted Mark. "You've cited the biggest problem that I have with faith—that it gets reduced to a transaction between me and God. I believe something and God rewards me with the biggest prize ever: eternal life. That's selfish, and it's just a repetition of everything our consumer society says: that we have to be compensated for everything. That's why I've had enough with the church."

"But is that it? Does that kind of transaction stand at the center of Jesus' preaching? Was that why Jesus came? I'm just not sure," sighed Angela. "Let's talk some more later." The two friends picked up their bags and headed for class. Angela was disappointed with Mark's response but also chagrined at the easy talk about eternal life that she had been hearing this week in church. What did it all mean? Did personal salvation stand at the center of Jesus' message?

Mark's response, though it might seem novel, has deep roots in critiques of Christian faith. Ludwig Feuerbach, a German philosopher who began his university studies training for the ministry, echoed similar sentiments nearly two hundred years ago. He claimed that Christian belief in eternal life could also be described in terms of the inestimable value that human beings place on their lives. We maintain that our lives are valuable, and the belief in everlasting life projects this value into eternity. Christian doctrines, for Feuerbach, pointed not to the things that human beings believed in but to human beings themselves, as believers. When we recognized this, Feuerbach claimed, we could finally be free, no longer dependent on God to act for us, grown-up enough to act for ourselves. Once liberated from the illusions of faith, human beings could focus more clearly on themselves and the betterment of this life.

What stands at the center of Christian hope? Is it belief in eternal life? Personal salvation? Or is it something broader and deeper? Do Mark and Feuerbach read Christian hope correctly? I claim in this chapter that Christian hope is more comprehensive than the question of our individual destinies. The proper way to begin our discussion of hope is with the image that occupies the center of Jesus' teaching and healing ministry: the kingdom of God. This kingdom that Jesus *proclaims and embodies* in his ministry grounds Christian hope not in individual matters but in communal relationships. Bearing witness to the kingdom that Jesus proclaimed, Christians widen the scope of hope to encompass the social and cosmic dimensions of life.

But what is the kingdom of God? Jesus never defines it in the Gospels. Instead, he *proclaims* it, *teaches* it in parables, and *embodies* it in his person. To comprehend the arc of Christian hope, we look first to the preaching, teaching, and healing ministry of Jesus of Nazareth.

A PROCLAMATION

New Testament scholars have become notorious in their arguments over the things that Jesus "really" said and did during his relatively brief ministry. Red-letter New Testaments notwithstanding, the words of Jesus are open to lively debate these days. Distinguishing the "real" words of Jesus from early Christian communities' remembrance of him and those words is thorny business. Amid this scholarly disagreement, however, is substantial agreement that Jesus proclaimed the kingdom of God, announcing a coming reign that would be revealed on earth. Jesus preached repentance and urged those who heard him to turn anew to the living God. In the Synoptic Gospels (Matthew, Mark, and Luke) Jesus talks very little about himself. His proclamation, rather, is other-directed, oriented toward the coming of a reign that belongs to God. This coming intervention and establishment of God's purposes on earth announces good news to a world wracked by sin. On Jesus' lips, the good news of the kingdom encompasses both judgment and hope. In the Gospel of Matthew, Jesus begins his public ministry on a note of warning: "Repent, for the kingdom of heaven has come near"[1] (Matt. 4:17b). This proclamation sets the tone for everything that follows in the Gospel, as Jesus gathers disciples who also bear witness to the imminence of God's reign. Without repentance, there is little hope, for without it one cannot inherit the kingdom.

Luke's Gospel offers further elaboration on the nature of the kingdom that Jesus proclaims: it begins in a synagogue and extends to the world's oppressed. In Luke, Jesus begins his public ministry by reading from a scroll of the prophet Isaiah, announcing good news to the poor, release to the captives, recovery of sight to the blind, and freedom to the oppressed (Luke 4:18). In doing so, he recalls the privilege that the Torah accorded to the widow, orphan, and resident alien. Jesus begins in the context of Jewish worship and in many respects remains there, at least figuratively, throughout Luke's narrative. (The disciples at the end of the Gospel, for example, are "continually in the temple blessing God" [24:53].) After reading from the scroll, Jesus performs several healings and tells the gathered masses, " 'I must proclaim the good news of the kingdom of God to the other cities also; for I was sent for this purpose.' So he continued proclaiming the message in the synagogues of Judea" (4:43–44).

As Christians remember and live into Jesus' proclamation of the kingdom, it is critical to remember that it began in the synagogue. In a day when many Christians ignore Jesus' Jewishness, the church must remember Jesus' proclamation of the kingdom as it connects with the hope of the prophets and God's covenant with Israel. Christian hope may expand that vision of the covenant, in the way that Isaiah does, but it ought not make the mistake that the church supplants the people Israel. Throughout its history, the church has often believed that it might save the covenant people through conversion to Christian faith. But such belief suggests that God forgets the promises made to Israel to remain faithful to God's people. The authentic hope unveiled in Jesus' proclamation of the kingdom, as it grows in the New Testament, is that even strangers to the covenant (Gentile Christians) might find a home in it. The good news of the kingdom is that we, as strangers, are grafted into that covenant: this is one of the "new things" that God is doing, which does not negate what God has been doing all along in covenant with Israel. Christians do not hope that all people will become Christian but that all might flourish as they are invited to participate in the covenant that God has established with God's people.

But what is the *content* of this proclamation of God's kingdom? What does Jesus say it is? What does it look like? Never does Jesus offer anything like a definition. Instead, Jesus proclaims the kingdom in images, stories, acts of healing, and gestures that grant privilege to outsiders. These actions and narratives give us some clues about the nature of this kingdom as it overturns the established, accepted order of things: socially, economically, and culturally. In Jesus' Sermon on the Plain, he says,

> "Blessed are you who are poor,
>   for yours is the kingdom of God.
> Blessed are you who are hungry now,
>   for you will be filled."
>   Luke 6:20–21

The kingdom, as it emerges from Jesus' lips and is proclaimed with his life, is not the continued validation of the present state of affairs but the inversion of it. Instead, Jesus calls his hearers to *repent* for the present order of things.

The kingdom he proclaims contains "nuisances and nobodies,"[2] where the poor, the suffering, children, widows, and strangers have special place. Hope in this framework is not chiefly for oneself (as Mark in the coffeehouse seems to think) but for *others*.

THE KINGDOM IN PARABLES

If Jesus refuses to define the kingdom, he offers multiple parables that invite us to imagine it. These parables resist tidy morals or sound bites that would condense Jesus' message. Some of the parables include explanations, such as the parable of the Sower (Matt. 13:1–23; Mark 4:1–20; Luke 8:4–15), but most of them do not. Jesus' parables, rather, allow the story to take root in the hearer, to invite those who listen to participate in the story itself and the coming of God's kingdom. Some of them call our attention to the excess within ordinary things. The kingdom of God is like a mustard seed that grows, becomes a tree, and a home for birds; or it is like yeast that leavens dough, causing increase (Matt. 13:31–33; Mark 4:30–32; Luke 13:18–21). Both of these comparisons call our attention to the mystery of growth, which cannot be attributed to our own efforts. Yeast and mustard grow rather profusely, without much regard for keeping their proper limits. The mustard seed can overtake the garden; the yeast causes the dough to rise beyond the container that houses it. There is something reckless about bountiful growth from insignificant beginnings. Though Jesus does not define the kingdom with such images, he indicates its abundance and disregard for keeping within polite norms. The kingdom of nuisances and nobodies is marked by excess; Christian hope is marked by its tendency to break boundaries of who is "in" and who is "out."

Meals, too, serve as parabolic examples of the kingdom in Jesus' teaching, especially meals that lack proper decorum. In the parable of the Great Dinner (Luke 14:15–24), a host prepares a great feast, invites many to dine, but all the invited guests have legitimate excuses not to attend, whether it is caring for their land, oxen, or spouse. After hearing their socially acceptable regrets, the host commands his slave to bring in the poor, crippled, blind, and lame. When the new guests arrive and room is still left at table, still others are brought to the feast. A strange banquet indeed, where those who are invited do not attend, where the forgotten have first seat at table, and others are compelled to partake of the feast. This meal stands on its head complacent understandings of whether one has been invited to attend or not. Christian hope for the kingdom is not the smug assurance that one knows that one is an honored guest, but hope that all will partake of the feast, even when those who are invited refuse to taste it. Hope is not for oneself but for others. In the economy of this banqueting table, Christians are both guests and hosts: guests at the table that the master has prepared in abundance; hosts because when we dine on the food and participate in the hospitality present at table, we also extend them to others. The parable of the Great Dinner transgresses the entrenched gulf between rich and poor, touchable and untouchable that permeates society. In the end, the house overflows, suggesting a kingdom that bursts with hospitality, even when we are not prepared to receive it.

If hope for the kingdom defies social custom in Jesus' parables, it also defies standard economic logic and our innate sense of fairness. In the parable of the Laborers in the Vineyard (Matt. 20:1–16), the landowner hires workers to tend his crop one morning, agreeing to pay them the usual wage for a day's work. But as the landowner sees others standing idle in the marketplace at midmorning, noon, and late afternoon, he hires them as well, as if to say, "There is more than enough work and wage to go around." At the end of the day, those who had been laboring since daybreak receive the same wage as those who were hired at 5 o'clock in the afternoon. Such behavior, glimpsed within a context of scarcity, is hardly good business practice; nor is it wise stewardship of one's resources. The landowner's actions defy fairness, but to those first hires who grumble, the landowner asks, "Are you envious because I am generous?" (v. 15). Again, the excessiveness of the parable is striking. Instead of holding on to what he has, the landowner gives it away, rather recklessly, upending the relationship between those who came first and those who arrive on the scene rather late.

In the kingdom of God, abundance rather than scarcity reigns. Christians have often believed and acted as if hope for the future were restricted to a select people. Throughout the ages, Christians have stated this idea in many ways: outside the church there is no salvation; heaven is only for the righteous; the Communion table is closed to all but a chosen few; strangers are not welcome here. When protective impulses impel us to draw lines of hope around ourselves, we contradict the movement of the parables. Whenever we construct circles to preserve righteousness, we wind up finding Jesus outside that circle, in solidarity with those who are excluded. In the reckless abundance of Christian hope, slackers and idlers earn a day's pay for an hour's worth of labor; strangers feast at table; and mustard seeds overtake the tidy garden. In the end, Christian hope is defined not by enclosing a few within a fence but in breaking the fence open so that all might come storming into the vineyard.

JESUS, EMBODIMENT OF THE KINGDOM

In his preaching and parables, Jesus proclaims the kingdom. He announces and anticipates God's reign, which is not yet fully present in the world. He calls his hearers to repentance so that the kingdom might break forth anew. Yet the Gospels do not simply portray the kingdom as a future aim; they point to the presence of the kingdom in the person of Jesus. Jesus, the proclaimer of God's reign, *is* God's reign. If we want to know what the kingdom looks like, we need look no further than him. In his acts of healing, blessing, and breaking bread, Jesus Christ embodies God's kingdom. The kingdom, in other words, comes not as a distant and disembodied ideal but in the healing, touching, feeding, and blessing of bodies.

Each of the Gospels portrays Jesus as a healer. Proclaiming the kingdom goes hand in hand with the new life borne of his touch: "When the crowds found out about it, they followed him; and he welcomed them, and spoke to them about the kingdom of God, and healed those who needed to be cured" (Luke 9:11). Jesus touches and heals bodies deemed unclean, particularly lepers. The disease of leprosy, in Jesus' time, was cause for social ostracism. When he touches lepers, Jesus does not simply cure a physical ailment; he heals bonds of society that have been broken because of fear and concern with purity. By touching lepers, he restores these broken bonds and gives new life—not only to lepers but to all who come into contact with him.

Yet the Gospels record not only Jesus' touch; they also portray others touching him. Others extend a hand to Jesus and find healing as well. The story of the hemorrhaging woman is particularly illustrative: "She had heard about Jesus, and came up behind him in the crowd and touched his cloak, for she said, 'If I but touch his clothes, I will be made well.' Immediately her hemorrhage stopped, and she felt in her body that she was healed of her disease" (Mark 5:27–29). Language of the body echoes loudly throughout this story: the woman reaches out to touch; Jesus at first is unaware but then senses her touch; the woman feels "in her body" that she was healed. Knowledge of the kingdom, accordingly, does not simply await us in the future; we also encounter it in the marrow of our bones in gestures of healing. Hope for the world comes in a touch that heals, known and experienced in bodies touched by grace.

Jesus' healing touch is also a movement of blessing. As he extends blessing in the name of the kingdom, he gathers more unexpected characters. At several points in the Gospels, children play significant roles. Luke's narration of one story is striking in its mention of touch and of those who receive the kingdom of God:

> People were bringing even infants to him that he might touch them; and when the disciples saw it, they sternly ordered them not to do it. But Jesus called for them and said, "Let the little children come to me, and do not stop them; for it is to such as these that the kingdom of God belongs. Truly I tell you, whoever does not receive the kingdom of God as a little child will never enter it." (Luke 18:15–17)

In Jesus' day as well as ours, the touch that children experience is often the hand of violence. In the face of such abuse, Jesus proclaims children as heralds of the kingdom. The inversion of social order is arresting: children belong not primarily to parents but to God and the community of faith, serving as exemplars of receiving the kingdom by grace. Jesus' proclamation and embodiment of the kingdom does not perpetuate the age-old structures of kingship—power, force, status—to which the world accustoms itself; instead, it overturns them. Jesus' kingdom is marked by vulnerability, hospitality, and peace, epitomized in a child touched by the Lord.

If the kingdom in Jesus Christ is touched and felt, the final chapters of the Gospels also remind us that it is *tasted*. Jesus appears often in the Gospels with food in his hands and wine in his cup. This occurs so frequently in his ministry that he is accused of being a glutton and drunkard (Matt. 11:19; Luke 7:34). The meals where Jesus appears as guest and host are marked by their excessiveness: he dines with the wrong kind of people at inopportune times. In his final meal, however, he embodies the feast of the kingdom most clearly. At the Supper, as he proclaims the cup as his blood and the bread as his body, he invites his disciples to taste the kingdom. Jesus invites his disciples to partake of the kingdom intimately, for taste is the most intimate form of touch. Jesus offers himself for the tasting and, in doing so, invites all who gather at table to taste the kingdom, not only in the bread and wine, but in how the meal is shared and given to the world. The excess of this meal is not its lavishness, for it is the simplest meal of all, comprised of the basic staple food, bread, and the basic drink of celebration, wine. Its excess is its intimacy and indiscriminate sharing, broken and given for all.

Jesus proclaims the kingdom as something yet to come, but he also embodies it in acts of healing, blessing, and table fellowship. As Christians yearn for Christ to come again, we do not simply stare into the far-off-distant future, we remember the future as we recall the person of Jesus Christ, who represents the coming of the kingdom. Christian hope is first and foremost grounded in celebration of the kingdom, a kingdom that subverts the very idea of kingship by extending its abundance to others.

QUESTIONS FOR DISCUSSION

1. Why do you think repentance is central to Christian hope?
2. What is your favorite parable? How does that parable illustrate the kingdom of God?
3. Describe a time when you have felt healing. How does that instance of healing relate to Christian hope?

3

The Resurrection of the Body

A week later, the coffeehouse conversation on Christian hope continues. It is still Easter season, and memories of the sermon on Christ's resurrection continue to rankle in Angela's brain: "The biggest problem I'm having with my parents' faith is this whole raising from the dead business. Of all Christian beliefs, this one requires the greatest leap. It flies in the face of our ordinary perceptions. When we die, we die: if we're buried, our bodies slowly decompose, fertilizing the soil that nourished our bodies while we were alive. To say that God raises bodies from the dead just seems weird."

"That's right," nodded Mark. "How many funeral visitations have you been to? The bodies that we see in those caskets are empty of life. I think a lot of Christian beliefs about the resurrection probably relate to our fear of death and our longing for those who've departed. We don't want our loved ones to leave us. So, what do we do? We console ourselves with the promise that we'll be reunited with them in heaven. It's all well-intentioned, but it doesn't have much grounding in reality."

"We're made from the dust of stars that exploded billions of years ago, and when we die, we turn to dust," assented Angela. "The only part of the Bible that deals with life and death frankly is Ecclesiastes: 'All go to one place; all are from the dust, and all turn to dust again' [Eccl. 3:20]."

RESURRECTION QUESTIONS

What do Christians mean by the resurrection? Angela and Mark are struggling with questions that multiple generations have asked. Questioning the

resurrection, even denying it, is hardly a new issue to Christian faith. The
New Testament records that the Sadducees, for example, claimed that there
was no resurrection (Mark 12:18). Given the fact that so many questions surround the resurrection, each generation in the faith, while listening to voices
that have gone before, has had to come to resurrection faith anew.

At death, our bodies and the bodies of all creatures return to the earth.
The life of our bodies is sustained by other living things that die, as we take
sustenance from the web of life on earth: fruits, grains, milk, and meat. When
we die, moreover, we fertilize the soil that nourished us while we were alive.
If belief in the resurrection means a cosmic exception to that cycle of life, a
miracle that zaps us out of the time-space continuum at the end of our days,
then that is simply something that most modern Christians cannot believe in.
Many squirm in their seats on Easter Sunday. Perhaps you do as well.

So what *do* Christians mean by the resurrection? Is it a belief about what
happens to the body? Is it a general affirmation on behalf of life? Is it wistful
longing for those who have departed? Is it a distraction from present, more
pressing concerns? In different respects, Christians throughout the ages have
answered questions about the resurrection along each of these lines. Mark
and Angela are hardly alone in asking hard questions about the resurrection.
Those questions have appeared ever since the discovery of the empty tomb,
and not simply by strangers to the faith. As John's Gospel reminds us, they
are asked by one of Jesus' own disciples, Thomas (John 20:24–29). If we claim
that one of the fundamental marks of Christian faith is that one cannot question the resurrection, then we depart from apostolic tradition. Questions
emerge at the beginning of the church's life. The first thing, therefore, to say
about the resurrection is that we should be wary of giving a final, definitive
answer about what it means. Indeed, nowhere in the New Testament do we
find anything that resembles an exhaustive description or definition.

Many Christians throughout the ages have stressed the miraculous nature
of the resurrection: it points to the reconstitution of our bodies either at
death or at the end of days. The medieval theologian Thomas Aquinas even
described what the risen body looked like. At the end of the age, resurrected
bodies would not exhibit varied forms (e.g., infant, youth, middle age, and
elderly) but one form, youth, which captures best the beauty and perfection of
the human form.[1] For Aquinas, there will be no osteoporosis in the resurrection, and we all will look like vigorous young adults! Other Christians, though
refraining from the specifics of the risen body, uphold the identity of the body
that has died with the risen flesh. According to the Westminster Confession,
one of the confessions of the Presbyterian Church, "the selfsame bodies of
the dead which are laid in the grave, being then again united to their souls
forever, shall be raised up by the power of Christ" (7.197). But Westminster

does not spell out what "selfsame" body means. During the Middle Ages and the Reformation period, as well as today, people were no less cognizant of the decay of flesh that accompanies death. Resurrection has always meant something different from the resuscitation of the human body.

Other Christians have shunned talk of a literal resurrection and opted instead for other interpretations. Twentieth-century theologian Rudolf Bultmann claimed that resurrection does not refer primarily to our destiny after the grave but concerns our coming to faith in the present moment. We awaken to resurrection as we are given new eyes to see in Christian faith: this applies to those early witnesses to the risen Christ as well as to us. The miracle is not what happens to earthly bodies but what happens in the life of faith. For Bultmann, we rise anew into resurrection when we live by faith, every day of our lives "and those who believe have already eternal life."[2] Many Christians these days inhabit the space between these ends of the spectrum, questioning the miraculous reconstitution of our bodies but remaining wary of reducing resurrection to a moment of faith. But what, then, *is* resurrection?

My first suggestion in interpreting resurrection faith is that we should refrain from claiming too much about it. Our lead should not be speculation about the next life and what it looks like but the rather sparse detail that the New Testament itself gives about the resurrection of Jesus. The resurrection, first and foremost, is not speculation about what happens to us after death; instead, it ought to relate to the primary focus of resurrection in the Bible: Jesus Christ.

BEDROCK OF CHRISTIAN FAITH

The birth of the church is bound up with resurrection. Women witness an empty tomb, disciples meet the risen Christ, and the claim of resurrection appears on the lips of his subsequent followers. Without some form of resurrection proclamation, the early Jesus movement would likely not have grown into the church; it probably would have been reabsorbed into the Judaism of its time. Paul offers one example of the centrality of resurrection for Christian faith. His transformative encounter with the gospel, according to Acts, is marked by bright light and a voice of the risen Christ (Acts 9:3–5). This appearance narrative signals Saul's conversion, his change from a persecutor of the Christian movement to its foremost apologist and evangelist: "If there is no resurrection of the dead, then Christ has not been raised; and if Christ has not been raised, then our proclamation has been in vain and your faith has been in vain" (1 Cor. 15:13–14).

For Paul, moreover, resurrection faith is not primarily about us and our destiny but about what occurs in and through Jesus Christ. Resurrection faith, moreover, concerns more than the question of what happened to Jesus' body after his death; it points to the life given to the world *through* Jesus Christ. Resurrection faith concerns itself with the body of Jesus of Nazareth, but it doesn't stop there. The resurrection is God's eternal validation of the life of Jesus; it is God's "yes" to Jesus, the kingdom he proclaims, the healing he enacts, the blessing that he confers, and the life he gives. As the Brief Statement of Faith puts it, "God raised this Jesus from the dead, vindicating his sinless life, breaking the power of sin and evil, delivering us from death to life eternal" (10.2). Resurrection faith tells us that life, not death, has the final word, and that we partake of this life most fully in Jesus.

Jesus confers resurrection life to us. For Paul, this link is critical. The Christian life, for him, is a sustained pattern of dying and rising with Christ: "For if we have been united with him in a death like his, we will certainly be united with him in a resurrection like his" (Rom. 6:5). For Paul, Christ is the pivot of history that frees us from sin: Jesus experiences the onslaught of the world's sin, dies on a cross because of sin, and rises from the grave in God's extension of grace. Christ is the "new Adam" who heals, reverses, and overcomes the reign of sin and death: "For since death came through a human being, the resurrection of the dead has also come through a human being; for as all die in Adam, so all will be made alive in Christ" (1 Cor. 15:21–22). To affirm the resurrection is to say yes to the incarnation, to what God is doing for the sake of the world's healing in Christ. In this sense, it has less to do with our supposed fear of death or with ego-boosting among Christians than it does about the new life and freedom from sin that God gives, day in and day out. Resurrection faith, first and foremost, is not belief in a cosmic miracle about what happens to dead flesh, but hope in God's purposes for the sake of the whole world in Jesus Christ. Hardly a selfish belief, it opens Christians to the beauty of the world and all bodies within that world.

AN AFFIRMATION OF BODIES

If the resurrection is God's yes to Jesus Christ, it is also God's yes to the body. Christianity, writes ecological theologian Sallie McFague, is the religion of embodiment par excellence. Our faith is saturated with imagery and affirmation of bodies. We proclaim Jesus of Nazareth as the incarnation, God's encounter with us in and through the body of a carpenter in first-century Galilee. Those who follow Christ make up his body, the Christian church. Week in and week out, Christians gather around the Lord's Table to celebrate a meal where we partake in Christ's body and blood. And we believe, in the words of the Apostles' Creed, "in the resurrection of the body" (2.3). One cannot be Christian without embracing the body.

In its earliest years, the church struggled with a movement known as Gnosticism that was popular in the Mediterranean world. Gnosticism offered a vision of eternal life that some Christians found attractive. But at its core, Gnosticism viewed the body as the fundamental problem of human existence and not part of its solution. For the Gnostics, our bodies were prisons that inhibited the flourishing of the divine spark that lay deeply embedded within each person. Human bodies and the body of creation were defective and needed to be overcome in order for the divine spark to spread and find salvation. The liberation of this spark, accordingly, could be found only through secret knowledge, or gnosis, that allowed the spark within us to rise to God and be reunited with its Maker. For Gnostics salvation meant a shunning of the body, as humans, through knowledge, cast aside bodily shackles in order that they might flourish. The Gnostics were suspicious of the body, relegating it, in the end, to destruction. Some early Christians saw affinities with a gnostic understanding of redemption and their own recognition of the fallen nature of all humanity. Christians were also aware of how persons were trapped, but for them, the trap was not *because* of the body but because of the sin that enslaved humanity, body and soul. Sin, rather than the body, presented the problem. Nonetheless, in some strands of the early church Christians exemplified sin with the desires of the body. Given this tendency, it is no surprise that Christian Gnosticism emerged. What kept early Christians from embracing Gnosticism was their insistence on the resurrection of the body. At the center of Christian hope, in other words, is a fundamental affirmation of the body: that God will not destroy the body on the road to redemption but preserve it for relationship with God.

For Christians, our relationship with God and our salvation occur not in spite of the body but because of it, for it is the body of Christ that gives us new life. As contemporary Reformed theologian Eugene Rogers has written, "The body is the way of the creature into the Triune God. Because in Jesus, God takes on a body to pave him the Way."[3] Hope for the world, salvation for all creation, comes in a God who takes the human body as God's own. A more resounding yes to human embodiment is hard to imagine, and that yes lies at the heart of resurrection faith.

A SPIRITUAL BODY

Resurrection faith, however, entails more than a general affirmation of bodies. If we affirm Jesus' resurrection, what kind of body are we affirming? Does it mean that Jesus' resurrected body is identical to his body as he lived in the first century? The New Testament clearly denies this correspondence. The risen Christ, in each of the Gospels, appears as a different sort of body. Jesus' own disciples, those whom he knew most closely, do not recognize him when he appears to them. They see him and talk with him, but they still do not see him for who he is. Their recognition occurs only when Jesus partakes in actions and gestures that recall his ministry, such as breaking bread (Luke 24:30–31) or calling them by name (John 20:16). The disciples recognize the risen body only when they sense its connection to Jesus' earthly body. But clearly, the resurrection body looks different, different enough to cause intimates not to recognize Jesus on first glance.

These resurrection stories suggest that the resurrection is not the miraculous reconstitution of each and every body part that compose our physiology. An affirmation of the body need not be confused with the idea that every cell, corpuscle, and platelet of Jesus' body—or ours—abides for eternity. Paul's terminology suggests a change in the body: "So it is with the resurrection of the dead. What is sown is perishable, what is raised is imperishable. . . . It is sown a physical body, it is raised a spiritual body" (1 Cor. 15:42–44). Christians need not maintain that resurrection faith is a cosmic exception to the processes of life and death, zapping us out of the time-space continuum for eternity. The resurrection affirms the body, but not as an identical body to the body that we experience in this life. The spiritual body is the body claimed, blessed, and redeemed by God.

The Gospels are silent about how the resurrection occurred. Between Jesus' burial and the discovery of the empty tomb, the Bible offers little besides a burial scene and the presence of friends who mourn—no descriptions of cosmic, divine intervention; no portrait of Jesus rising from the grave (in contrast to the innumerable paintings and icons that pepper church walls throughout history); no narration of resurrection miracle. Descriptions of the resurrection exist in Christian literature, but they are extracanonical. I don't think this is coincidence. Resurrection faith, at its most basic level, is not about describing in detail what happened to Jesus on the third day. The church—most of the time—has been content simply confessing, along with the Nicene Creed, "on the third day he rose again according to the Scriptures" (1.2) and that is certainly enough.

A well-known joke postulates that archaeologists discover bones in Jerusalem that can definitively be identified as Jesus' own. Jerry Falwell is notified and cries out, "This is disastrous news. Christian faith will surely crumble." The pope finds out and ponders, "Let me summon my foremost theologians to investigate these claims." Rudolf Bultmann hears the news and quips, "Ach, dere really vas a Jesus." Would such a discovery, if ever "proven,"[4] amount to a fatal torpedo shot at the ship of Christian faith? If the resurrection is simply about what happens to Jesus' body, then, yes. But if it is about something more, about God's validation of what is happening in Jesus Christ and what it means for our lives, body, and soul, then such a discovery, however initially shocking, could not shake the core of resurrection faith. "What is sown is perishable, what is raised is imperishable" (1 Cor. 15:42). The risen body is different from the bodies that we know and touch here and now, but it remains a body, a body made for communion with God.

A WOUNDED BODY

One other detail about the Gospel narratives of Jesus' resurrection appearance is interesting and often overlooked: the risen Christ reveals his wounds. Resurrection does not erase the scars of crucifixion but preserves them. The doubting Thomas story offers the clearest indication of this detail, as Jesus invites Thomas to put his hands inside Jesus' wounds. This invitation, this touch of a tear in Jesus' side, opens Thomas's eyes to the reality of resurrection: "'My Lord and my God!'" (John 20:28). The wounds of Jesus are present but do not cause pain. How is this detail significant for Christian faith? I want to make one suggestion: the resurrection does not erase the scars, injustice, and pain of history. Some have portrayed the resurrection as a kind of ultimate happy ending, as if resurrection faith amounted to historical amnesia, where all the tragedy and negativity of history will be forgotten. But such a vision contravenes the testimony of Jesus and Thomas: in Jesus' body the wounds of his crucifixion are remembered.

History, as we well know, is typically the story of those who triumph. The voices we read from the past are generally not those who have been trampled upon, oppressed, and systematically executed, but resurrection faith remembers them, hearing "the voices of peoples long silenced" (10.4). To claim the resurrection of the dead is to claim that the dead, too—all of them—continue to have voice, somehow, some way, in the mystery of God's eternal presence and grace. In the resurrection, though pain and mourning reign no more, nothing is forgotten or obliterated but gathered together into God's very life. Part of the good news of resurrection faith is that God does not erase the world's wounds but remembers them in the resurrection body so that they no longer cause suffering. The risen body is not the perfect specimen of youth, as Thomas Aquinas portrayed it, but witnessed in different bodies, each bearing wounds uniquely their own.

INDIVIDUALITY OR ITS DISAPPEARANCE?

Each human life is unique: uniquely given by God, uniquely blessed with particular gifts and experiences. Resurrection faith affirms this uniqueness. If nothing is forgotten in the resurrection, then our individuality does not disappear at the end of days. Some visions of redemption and salvation maintain that eternal life erases our uniqueness. Some popular conceptions describe our destiny as a drop of water returning to the ocean. In the new life, the self (the drop of water) relinquishes its identity and returns to its source; the self, in this sense, disappears.

One of the fundamental differences between Christianity and some Eastern religions concerns how they respectively understand the endurance or disappearance of individuality. For Buddhists, Christians seem to clutch their individuality stubbornly, refusing to let go; while for Christians, Buddhists relinquish too quickly the uniqueness of each self. Clearly, for Christians, the self often presents itself as problematic; one of the classic understandings of sin is the overzealous assertion of the self against others and God. But the healing from sin, in most Christian understandings, does not entail the letting go of self but its healing and transformation in relation to God by grace. Those who witness the appearance of the risen Christ eventually recognize him and relate to him. Christ's resurrection preserves something about Christ's individuality, however elusive and mysterious it is. As those who live in light of resurrection, our identity is also preserved, now and for all time. To live in relation to another, after all, assumes that we do not disappear into that other.

IMMORTALITY OF THE SOUL?

Is a Christian understanding of resurrection similar to a belief in the immortality of the soul? Sometimes Christians use these terms interchangeably, but there are important differences between them. Many religions throughout history have stressed the soul's immortality: the idea was present long before Christian faith emerged, and it gained wide acceptance in the Greek world of Jesus' time. The idea of the soul's immortality is chiefly a belief about *us*: a part of us, dubbed the soul, is indestructible and will endure throughout all time. There is something special about this soul that makes it worthy of living forever. Christian belief in the resurrection, however, says something different: it reflects not a belief about *us* but about *God* and what God is doing in each and every life. The resurrection claims not that some part of us is entitled to live forever but that God brings life out of death and is continually creating new life.

The idea of the soul's immortality is problematic for other reasons. When Christians separate the soul from the body, they often value the soul more than the body: the soul is "spiritual" while the body is merely "physical." This split between soul and body, if accompanied by such value judgments, actually runs counter to resurrection faith. As a faith that stresses embodiment, Christianity views soul and body together. The soul is the *life* of the body, not separate from the body. As living beings, we are embodied souls or ensouled bodies, made for communion with God. The problem, in other words, is not with the distinction between body and soul; it's with how some have interpreted the distinction to mean the value of one part of humanity over another. The Reformed confessions, in general, do not value soul over body. As an example, take the Westminster Confession: "The bodies of men, after death, return to dust, and see corruption, but their souls . . . immediately return to God who gave them. . . . At the last day . . . the dead shall be raised up with the self-same bodies, and none other, although with different qualities, which shall be united again to their souls forever" (6.177–78). Soul and body belong together.

Christian belief in the resurrection of the body is not synonymous with the immortality of the soul. Resurrection unites body and soul in new life given by God. This belief stems not from an irrational fear of death but grows out of hope for life in its fullness. The resurrection, in other words, confirms what Christians already say about creation: that all of life is intended for God, in praise and glory to the Creator. Resurrection brings creation to fruition, its new beginning in God's very life. As the Presbyterian Confession of 1967 puts it, "The resurrection of Jesus is God's sign that he will consummate his work of creation and reconciliation beyond death and bring to fulfillment the new life begun in Christ" (9.26). Resurrection is what God intends for *all* life in the cosmos.

ETERNAL LIFE OR LIVING FOREVER?

The coffee-house conversation posed at the beginning of this chapter offers a common understanding of Christian hope. We do not want to die; nor do we want anyone whom we love to die. Christians hope, therefore, for a reunion with all their loved ones in heaven, where they will live forever, never missing another person because of death. In heaven, we will strum harps, see our friends, and praise God forever. Such understandings of resurrection life, however, merely take our experiences of time and life and graph them onto eternity. Does resurrection life equate with living forever? There are problems if it does: First, it is unclear whether "living forever" is even desirable.

Many visions of hell, for example, contain images of people doing the same tasks over and over, without end. If heaven involves ceaseless harp playing, that may be comforting to harp virtuosos but hardly desirable for the rest of us—and even for harpists it may soon prove monotonous. This popular vision of resurrection life, in other words, is a long, drawn-out vision of this life.

Life eternal, rather, is *not* the same as living forever. It is instead the *fulfillment* of our lives, reached in communion with God. We do not know what this looks like, but we can say that it's not simply extending forever the cycle of time as it applies to our lives. Otherwise, heaven becomes one damn thing after another. Life eternal describes not the endless experience of time but the glorification of our lives in relation to God, in and through the body. It's about *relationship* more than time, a relationship that begins *now*. Here is how the Confession of 1967 puts it: "Life in Christ is life eternal" (9.26). The Bible is short on detail in respect to life eternal but long on hope for it. Eternal life indicates, again, not something within us that endures but something that God is doing in us and in the world. Long as we might for a blueprint of this life, none is given, for the blessedness of this fulfilled life, this relationship, is something "which no eye has seen, nor ear heard, nor the heart of man conceived" (Heidelberg Catechism, 4.058). Living forever merely extends our understanding of earthly life, while eternal life embraces the life of the world as a gift from God. Eternal life is the fulfillment of human life in love, the everlasting dance of love that is God's life for the world. The good news is that as our lives are fulfilled by God's grace, we become fitted for participation in that love eternally.

RESURRECTION IN THE PRESENT

Because God has raised Christ from the dead, we not only anticipate resurrection at the end of life but experience it as the gathered people of God. Resurrection is a *present* as well as future reality. The Gospel of John is particularly emphatic on this point. In the story of Lazarus, for example, Jesus tells Martha, "'I am the resurrection and the life. Those who believe in me, even though they die, will live, and everyone who lives and believes in me will never die'" (John 11:25–26). Note how present *and* future tenses inform each other here: Jesus *is* the resurrection, and those who follow and believe in him will live. The entire scope of the church's liturgical practice reminds us of these connections between past, present, and future: in baptism, we die and rise with Christ; at the Eucharist we recall Jesus' final meal, while participating in and longing for the heavenly banquet. Christians *already* experience resurrection in Jesus Christ, as the new people created by the waters of second birth, baptism; but we also long for resurrection as the consummation of the world and the coming of God's reign.

Because Jesus is risen, Christians do not simply await the new life that he gives. God gives it to us right here, right now. As the Heidelberg Catechism notes, "First, by [Christ's] resurrection he has overcome death that he might make us share in the righteousness which he has obtained for us through his death. Second, we too are *now* raised by his power to a new life" (4.045, my emphasis). Christian belief in the resurrection, if we follow this lead, is not an opiate of the masses, promising folks who suffer to resign themselves to status quo injustice in the promise of a better world after death. Rather, it is an invitation to receive the abundance of life now and to be gathered into God's labors on behalf of life: labors for justice and for peace. Resurrection faith does not so much console the suffering as it empowers them for new life here, now, and into the future. In Christ, life—not death—has the final cosmic word. The fact that each of us is created from the dust of exploding stars and returns to dust at death only adds, rather than detracts, from the mystery of resurrection faith and the mystery of life.

QUESTIONS FOR DISCUSSION

1. How, in your experience, has Christian faith affirmed the goodness of the body? How has it denied that goodness?
2. Is it important, or not, to make a distinction between eternal life and living forever?
3. How can we continue to pay attention, in church and society, to those who have died? How can we take their voices seriously?
4. How does Christian belief in the resurrection affect our mourning of those who have died?

4

A Second Coming
in Judgment and Grace

Soon after I began graduate studies in theology, my next-door neighbor discovered what I intended on doing "for a living." An eager conversationalist, avid grower of orchids, parent of young children, and physician, he was also intrigued that someone could earn one's daily bread by teaching, thinking, and writing about Christian faith. He was also a skeptic. Sometimes I would come home from the library and find him puttering around in his front yard. Whenever this occurred, he would say something like, "What's God up to today, Dave?" These good-natured quips were meant to invite my response, and usually they did. Our conversations over the two years we were neighbors ranged over all kinds of topics, and many of the details have now faded from memory, but one conversation in particular sticks out. In it our thoughts wandered to the afterlife. I remember his saying something like this: "It seems to me, Dave, that Christian faith is pretty simple. You all believe that the Son of God came to earth, lived, taught, died, and rose from the grave. And you also claim that this Son of God will return someday. When he comes again, the good people will be saved and the bad folks will be judged unworthy. So, the motivation is to be a good person, have faith, and be on God's side. The reward for being good is heaven when Christ comes again; the punishment for being bad is hell. That's what it boils down to for me."

I remember his words more than mine during that conversation. At the time I was wondering myself what Christian faith "boils down to." Many persons, skeptics as well as devout believers, hold a similar view of the "essence" of Christian faith. One day a Judge will return to hold all people accountable for their actions, rewarding the righteous and punishing the wicked. After I moved from one student apartment to another on a different side of town, I lived a block away from a fundamentalist church whose parishioners engaged in door-to-door proselytizing. One day a member of this church handed me a tractate complete with cartoon character representations of Jesus' return in glory, the blessed in heaven, and the tormented in hell. Perhaps you have seen or read a similar pamphlet. At the end of this tractate was a brief prayer, which offered those who prayed it in sincerity the promise of eternal life. This pious tractate and my skeptical neighbor actually held similar views of the essence of Christian faith, centered on a heavenly Jesus who returns to earth to judge the living and the dead. They also share in common the assumption that Christian faith is chiefly *personal*: the central motivation for faith is the concern over what will happen *to me* after death, when Christ returns. Common as this view is, it represents a departure—and even a distortion—of Christian faith from a Reformed point of view. Contrary to tractates and my neighbor's lively words, the return of Christ in glory is not chiefly about me and whether I deserve reward or punishment; it's about the establishment of God's justice in the world. Christian belief in Christ's "second coming" is a social rather than personal posture. Indeed, the only place in Scripture where the term "personal" occurs is in an unflattering light: "A fool takes no pleasure in understanding, but only in expressing personal opinion" (Prov. 18:2). As people who anticipate Christ's return, we relish this life, living not in fear of judgment but assured that God's justice will be revealed to all peoples.

"GREAT IS THE MYSTERY OF FAITH"

To their credit, my skeptical neighbor and the cartoon-filled tractate were emphatic about one essential point: central to Christian faith is the hope that Christ will come again. The One who lived, preached, healed, was crucified and buried, and rose from the dead has not disappeared from history. He will come again, not as a stranger but as One who already knows us. This hope sustained the earliest Christians and continues to sustain the church in the present day: the last word in the universe is not the whimper of a world in the throes of death but a Savior who brings new life when he comes again. What does this "second coming" mean? When Christians celebrate the Lord's Supper, they recite these words that are shared across denominations—Catholic, Reformed, Lutheran, Anglican, Methodist, and countless others: "Great is the mystery of faith: Christ has died, Christ is risen, Christ will come again." Note how each verb in this phrase points to a different dimension of time: the mystery of faith pervades the past (Christ has died), present (Christ is risen), and future (Christ will come again). As we begin to interpret Christ's return, we must continually be aware of its connection to Christ's life and death and his continued presence here and now. Christian hope in Christ's return is not simply forward-looking; it encompasses all of time, as Christ is the Lord of time.

To claim that Christ will come again, therefore, is more than saying yes to the idea that at some future point in time Jesus will descend from the heavens and return to earth in glory. It is, rather, to be caught up in the new life that the risen Christ gives to the world day after day, knowing that this life is the beginning of the kingdom of God. The One whom we await, therefore, comes anew every day, bringing life out of death, hope out of despair. Karl Barth, the most influential Reformed theologian of the twentieth century, claimed that we cannot understand the final return of Christ apart from the resurrection and the sending of the Holy Spirit at Pentecost. If we do otherwise, we separate the expectation of Christ's return from the two fundamental experiences of new life in the church: Christ's return, in other words, is not the only eschatological event that gives hope; so, too, are resurrection and the gift of the Holy Spirit. As Christians hope for the coming of Christ, therefore, they also look to Easter and Pentecost. In this sense, the last days occur not merely on the far horizon of time but in the midst of the church's year, for Christ comes again at Pentecost and Easter year after year.

A KINGDOM HIDDEN ON EARTH

The Christian church has often focused on the future at the expense of the present. This was true in John Calvin's day as much as our own. During Calvin's lifetime, like ours, the violence of society was appalling. Wars of religion ravaged Europe; Christians slew other Christians in the name of a purified faith. This bloodbath produced no shortage of prophets predicting the imminent return of Christ as Lord, even speculations about the date of his return. In the midst of their speculations, Calvin warned against apocalyptic fervor. His focus on the hope of Christ's return also turned attention squarely toward *this life*: "Christ gives to his own people clear testimonies of his very present power. Yet his Kingdom lies hidden in the earth, so to speak, under the lowness of the flesh. It is right, therefore, that faith be called to ponder that visible presence of Christ which he will manifest on the Last Day" (*Institutes* 2.16.17). Anticipation of Christ's return, for Calvin, was closely connected to the *present* power of Christ's kingdom that often lies hidden to all but the eyes of faith. Anticipating Christ's return did not mean that Christians would sit idly but that they would embrace the present gift of power and life in Christ. If we regard Christ's return as a dramatic special-effects show, we disconnect Christ's return from his incarnation and resurrection. If the second coming recalls the first, then we should also expect Christ to appear in unexpected and neglected spaces, in solidarity with the victims of injustice rather than in thunderbolts of kingly might. For when the Son of God, herald of the kingdom, came, most people ignored, rejected, or despised him. They did not recognize him for who he was. If we "remember the future,"[1] then Christ's advent should recall his incarnation. To claim, with Calvin, that the kingdom of Christ is often hidden is to point to the way in which God's justice unfolds: in weakness rather than strength (1 Cor. 1:25); in vulnerability rather than triumph; in solidarity with the victims rather than in glory with the victors. God's justice does not perpetuate the never-ending struggle of might in the name of right; it uplifts the oppressed and calls the oppressors to account, not so that some may be rewarded and others punished but so that all might partake in the fullness of God's kingdom. Christ returns for nothing less than this.

THE ESTABLISHMENT OF JUSTICE IN A STRANGE JUDGMENT

Belief in Christ's return focuses on justice. We live in a world where injustice seems to reign. The earth's fields and farms produce enough to feed the world, yet their bounty is not shared. Wars rage in nearly every corner of the globe. A heralded age of globalization that promises prosperity to all only widens the gulf between rich and poor. Our attempts at implementing justice, moreover, often fail. Remedies for injustice include trials and prison sentences, but the wealthiest perpetrators of injustice often avoid their just desserts. Meanwhile, incarceration rates for the poor and racial ethnic minorities escalate. Young black males are more visible in jails than on university campuses. Construction of more prisons continues unabated in the United States, demonstrating Americans' sense of insecurity. The world, no doubt, cries out for justice. How does Christian belief in Christ's return affect our understanding of justice and its implementation?

Judgment and justice have figured prominently since the earliest days of the Christian church. Judgment continues to loom large in many popular understandings of Christian faith: at the end of days the just will receive their reward while the guilty will get what they deserve. But if judgment is central to Christian understandings of Christ's return, it reveals itself strangely. This judgment does not focus on who deserves what, but on the establishment of God's justice, a justice that comes by God's transforming grace. This One who comes again is the person who takes whatever judgment we deserve upon himself, renewing all creatures and rendering our accounts about who is deserving and who is undeserving as illegitimate.

Let me put it bluntly: my neighbor was wrong. Christian hope is not about the just getting their desserts. The Reformers knew this rather well. In the face of an elaborate system of penance that specified how one could compensate for sin and merit forgiveness, they claimed that all of God's grace, all of God's gifts, were unearned. When Christ comes again in glory to judge, it will not be to label some as meritorious and others as not. As the Westminster Confession puts it, the point is "for the manifestation of the glory of his mercy in the eternal salvation of the elect" (6.181). The point, in other words, is to show God's grace in establishing justice for salvation: God's desire for all things to gain life in its abundance in and through God. God's justice reestablishes relationships broken by sin and violence: This is what "communion" means. To separate oneself from this communion is death; to live in and through it is life.

What does Christ judge in his return? Prominent in the book of Revelation is the figure of Babylon, an image that most scholars take as referring to the Roman Empire. In New Testament times, Rome was *the* empire, extending its cultural, economic, and political influence through colonization, trade, and military conquest. Jesus lived as a colonized person of this empire. All roads, in his day, truly led to Rome. But this unquestioned authority of the empire is what Revelation judges as bankrupt, destined for demise. This luxurious city has now become a "dwelling place of demons, a haunt of every foul spirit" (Rev. 18:2). Babylon's merchants "were the magnates of the earth, and all nations were deceived by [their] sorcery" (18:23). Yet their economic might is ephemeral: "Alas, alas, the great city, where all who had ships at sea grew rich by her wealth! For in one hour she has been laid waste" (18:19). Why is Babylon singled out for judgment? Part of the answer, I would claim, lies in how Babylon (Rome) extends the benefits of its economic and political might, where some "earn" blessing while others do not. While merchants grew fat by the dint of their economic labors, others labored to fill the merchants' coffers; while an empire grew under the march of a military boot, hundreds of thousands were colonized as their just desserts. The problem of mercantile acquisition, the problem of empire, is its rationalization that some merit blessing while others do not; this is the very thing that incurs judgment on Christ's return. However human beings attempt to divide the population into deserving and undeserving masses incurs the judgment of the One who comes in grace.

In the extreme reach of empire, even violence is justified in establishing imperial aims. The book of Revelation is no stranger to violence: present on nearly every page is an image of the destructive effects of violence. Some have argued that Revelation assumes violence in the present order, even justifying it in the name of the righteous. I read it alternatively: the book actually subverts violence in its image of a slain and nonviolent Lamb who returns as the Redeemer of the world. But if Revelation understands the second coming nonviolently, it is also aware of those who bear the scars of Babylon's violence. Any accounting of hope in Christ's return must grapple with the violence that so often reigns in the present day. The Scots Confession states this hope in the face of violence succinctly:

> We believe that the same Lord Jesus shall visibly return for this Last Judgment as he was seen to ascend. And then, we firmly believe, the time of refreshing and restitution of all things shall come, so that those who from the beginning have suffered violence, injury, and wrong, for righteousness' sake, shall inherit that blessed immortality promised them from the beginning. (3.11)

Central to this vision of final judgment is not the bestowing of reward and punishment but the remembrance of violence inflicted against the victims of history. The aim of hope is not the further triumph of the victorious but the "refreshing" of those who bear the brunt of the world's violence. Christ's return does not mean that the world forgets violence or overcomes it with more violence, but that divine justice is for the sake of life, not death.

The justice of the coming Lord is not a mirror of the justice that often proceeds in most corners of the world, where the guilty are punished and the innocent compensated. Those visions of justice are merely partial in trying to amend the damage done to creation through injustice. The justice of the kingdom, by contrast, aims at restoring communities to wholeness. In this vision, the perpetrators of injustice are called to account—by hearing the voices of the oppressed—and come face-to-face with the victims of their actions, summoned to recognize the humanity of the persons they treated as inhuman. Here the oppressed are finally allowed to speak without interference, to be heard into their humanity, and in the process even to recognize the humanity of their oppressors. Such a vision, moreover, recognizes that we are almost never only an oppressor or a victim, for one of the pernicious effects of sin is that victims of sin often wind up victimizing others. This process of restorative, transformative justice is not brief; it takes more than a lifetime and is possible only by the grace of the One who has already taken the "deserved" judgment upon himself.[2]

Given this vision of justice, are we, then, to quiver before the promise of Christ's return? The book of Revelation offers a picture of the Last Judgment that ends not with fear but with hope:

> And let everyone who is thirsty come.
> Let anyone who wishes take the water of life as a gift.
>   Rev. 22:17

We live as people of hope because the judgment we deserve has already been embodied in Jesus Christ. The Confession of 1967 bears witness to this hope:

> Jesus Christ is the judge of all men. His judgment discloses the ultimate seriousness of life and gives promise of God's final victory over the power of sin and death. . . . All who put their trust in Christ face divine judgment without fear, for the judge is their redeemer. (9.11)

The strange judgment of the Last Judgment is that the just don't get their desserts; rather, God's justice in grace transforms all people for the sake of communion. Jesus bears in his body all the violence of a sin-sick world, remembering every act of economic, physical, and social violence that infects the world—both the acts that we commit and those that are inflicted upon us. We live not in fear that those acts have the final word, nor in the fear that we will be punished for them, but in the hope that God's justice calls us all to account. Grace, in this vision, does not cancel out justice but makes justice transformative. God's justice in the Last Judgment doesn't simply restore what has been lost because of violence and sin but shapes us for relationship with God and one another.

Christian hope calls for resistance against all powers that demean, dehumanize, and enslave. Working for justice, we bear witness to the coming Lord, anticipating the kingdom that comes by his grace. In this vision of justice, all life belongs to God. The Barmen Declaration, a confession forged in the struggle against Nazism, notes, "We reject the false doctrine, as though there were areas of our life in which we would not belong to Jesus Christ, but to other lords—areas in which we would not need justification and sanctification through him" (8.15). In stating Christ as the Lord of all life—past, present, and future—this confession encourages us not merely to await the coming of the Lord, but empowers Christians to resist those who claim to be lord.

WHEN WILL THAT DAY COME?

A question lingering on the edges of this chapter, for many no doubt, is the question of timing: when will the Last Judgment occur? The minute we start framing the question this way, however, we are on the road to the wrong answers. Jesus, by contrast, offers some fairly clear words on this subject: "'But about that day and hour no one knows, neither the angels of heaven, nor the Son, but only the Father'" (Matt. 24:36). Jesus, in other words, does not know the time of his return. Christians live as a hopeful people not by speculating about a definitive time and place but by pointing in word and deed to the reign of God Christ promises and embodies. Whenever healing counters violence, whenever love overcomes hatred, whenever the hungry are fed, whenever we discover beauty in the midst of the grotesque, Christians anticipate the coming of the Lord and live as eschatological people. Christians live as though prepared for that day not only in their waiting but by witnessing to Christ's lordship in every facet of life.

Warnings about an imminent end or wariness over signs of the time may in fact point to hope in something *other* than Christ, as Jesus warned: "'For many will come in my name, saying, "I am the Messiah!" and they will lead many astray. And you will hear of wars and rumors of wars; see that you are not alarmed; for this must take place, but the end is not yet'" (Matt. 24:5–6). Christians best anticipate the future return of Christ by recalling the circumstances of his first coming. In his preaching, Jesus of Nazareth proclaimed much on behalf of God and others but little on behalf of himself. In his acts of healing, he cured disease and restored persons to communion, but he did so without fanfare or acclamation. The recurring theme throughout his ministry was humility and, in the end, even rejection. Christ's return, despite the legions of tractates to the contrary, does not simply extend judgment as a king on a throne but as a slain Lamb who comes as servant of all. Strange judgment indeed.

EXCURSUS: CHRISTIAN HOPE AND MODERN SCIENCE

In Petersburg, Kentucky, one can visit a museum built by a group of Christians that documents the age of the earth based on a "biblical worldview." In it, visitors find out through various exhibits that the fossils of dinosaurs are not millions of years old, as carbon dating suggests. Rather, dinosaurs once roamed the earth with primitive human beings. Through a literal reading of the Genesis creation story, and by extrapolating the dates of the generations of families recorded in Genesis, the founders of this museum have arrived at an approximate age of the earth: six thousand years. By contrast, the best estimates of mainstream science—astrophysics and evolutionary biology—point to a vastly more ancient cosmos. The universe came into being between ten and fifteen billion years ago; the earth dates back some four billion years, while modern human beings have emerged only within the last 120,000 years, a mere blip of cosmic time. We appear very late on the scene, to say the least. The museum in Kentucky, when faced with these data and discoveries, raises an adamant "No" to the conclusions of modern science. If the Bible "tells" us that the earth is six thousand years old and science suggests otherwise, then the scientists must be wrong, and any archaeological, geological, or astronomical discovery made must be false or made to conform to biblical "truths." On the other side, many who want to uphold the integrity of scientific investigation assume that if one accepts the scientific account of cosmic emergence, the biblical stories must be wrong. For both of these camps, the choice is clear: either science or Scripture.

The biblical writers, no doubt, shared the worldviews of their respective eras. Their understanding of the earth's age was surely less than four billion years, and they, like many subsequent generations, would have believed that the sun revolved around the earth. When Jesus walked along the shore of the Sea of Galilee and gazed up at the stars, he, like Moses, Augustine, and St. Francis, would have assumed that the stars were points of celestial light rotating around us in set orbits. To suggest otherwise would have seemed absurd.

Given the dissonance between ancient and modern understandings of the heavens and the age of the earth, how should Christians understand the "end of the world" in light of Christ's return? As a blueprint? As a cloud of glory that will mark the end of the entire universe? Modern science tells us that solar systems, galaxies, and the universe itself are in a constant flux of evolution. You, me, and all things on planet earth were gestated from the dust of exploding stars eons ago. At some point in the distant future, our sun, too, will die out, either in a supernova or diminishment into a dwarf star. Whether with a bang or a whimper, the solar system and life as we know it will cease to exist. Yet the ashes of our solar system will fuel the emergence of energy and matter elsewhere in the cosmos. Just because human life ends, just because the life of our solar system ends, that doesn't mean cosmic life ceases. To think otherwise is to put ourselves, rather than the universe itself, at the center of things. Are supernovas and the return of Christ as Lord, then, antithetical to one another?

As one of my colleagues has put it, we must opt for one narrative over another only if we consider eighth-grade earth science to be a threat to faith. And if that is the case, the God of Christian faith is too small. The Reformed tradition, however, sees the relationship between science and faith differently. One of the marks of this tradition, as Brian Gerrish has noted, is that it is "open to wisdom and truth wherever they are to be found."[3] Calvin drew on the humanist classics—Aristotle as well as the Bible—in formulating theology for his time. The "truth" of Scripture is not meant to be seen in contrast to "truth" discovered by scientific investigation. If it really is God's universe, then we ought, like Calvin, to see nature and the universe as the theater of God's glory. There is no place in the universe that we ought not investigate and learn more about; and in learning and discovering, we grow in our knowledge of God's world.

If this is the case, then we ought *not* read narratives of Christ's return—or creation stories for that matter—as blueprints for what will occur or scientific records of what has occurred. They are stories not of *description* but of *orientation*. They do not describe chiefly how the world came into being and how it will end, but they orient persons toward God and claim that God is the ultimate ground of all creation. When we read in Revelation about the return of Christ, we should not understand it as a movie script for future events that will unfold exactly along the lines of the story; rather, they are stories—like the stories of creation in Genesis—that anchor our hope in the God who is the source of all things and the aim of all things in Jesus Christ. Sustained by these biblical stories, science appears not as a threat but as further testimony to the mystery of God's world. How amazing that you, I, and all life on earth were formed from the dust of exploding stars and all that we know on this planet will also return to the universe as matter and energy at death and the death of our solar system! The fact that you and I, ferns and fauns, amoebas and anemones, are here at all is more than enough food to last a lifetime of thought and investigation, unto the end of the world as we know it.

THE LAST JUDGMENT AND EARTHLY GRATITUDE

By now it should be clear that Christians, in this understanding of the Last Judgment, do not live as hopeful people by turning their eyes toward the sky, waiting for Jesus to descend from the clouds. We do not count this life as loss in our anticipation of whatever lies ahead. Life on earth, in this understanding, is not a way station to a better world. Rather, one lives as a hopeful person in anticipation of Christ's return by giving thanks for this life and relishing all the good within it. Instead of focusing on the clouds, Christians hope by turning to the world (clouds included!) in its majesty and glory, its cries for justice, its call for our labors. In the middle of his meditation on future life, Calvin stresses the bounty of this life and thankfulness for life. Our understanding of life should engender

> no hatred of it or ingratitude against God. . . . Indeed, this life, however crammed with infinite miseries it may be, is still rightly counted among those blessings of God which are not to be spurned. Therefore, if we recognize in it no divine benefit, we are already guilty of grave ingratitude toward God himself. (*Institutes* 3.9.3)

Those who hate life contradict the main chords of Christian hope. Those who do not enjoy the gifts of life are witnesses against Christ's return.

In the first century, Jesus' enjoyment of life aroused suspicion, earning him the label of a glutton and a drunkard (Matt. 11:19). Those who called him these names, however, misunderstood him: Jesus' relishing of this life was testament to his promise of life eternal. Contrary to the caricatures that depict Calvin as a killjoy who despised all physical enjoyments, Calvin also found pleasure in the good things of the earth and the work of human hands. Listen to his words on food and clothing: "Now if we ponder to what end God created food, we shall find that he meant not only to provide for necessity but also for delight and good cheer. Thus the purpose of clothing, apart from necessity, was comeliness and decency" (*Institutes* 3.10.2). The physical pleasure of eating a tasty meal and the beauty of clothes woven and dyed by human hands are good things of life for which we give thanks. In themselves, they are worthy of our appreciation and enjoyment, not merely because they point to the Creator but because they are good *as they are*. Christians live as a hopeful people by enjoying and giving thanks every day.

It is no coincidence that one of the chief metaphors for Christ's return is a wedding banquet: a meal that does not simply fill the belly with nutrients but also delights the eye, pleases the tongue, and welcomes new members to the family. At wedding banquets—if they are ones that are truly celebratory—there is always more than enough food to go around, more than enough cheer, more than enough hope. In Jesus' parable of the Ten Bridesmaids (Matt. 25:1–13), those who are ready are invited into the banquet. The warning at the end is for the reader to keep awake, "'for you know neither the day nor the hour'" (v. 13). That which we await is not a judgment of terror but a feast like no other, prepared by a host who has already taken the world's judgment upon himself. If Christians anticipate this meal, they also give thanks for each daily meal, enjoying the nourishment—as well as the celebration and communion—that is present whenever food is shared.

WHO GETS INVITED?

Who, in the end, gets invited to the banquet? If the judgment of God is for the sake of communion, in contrast to all the ways people separate the deserving from the undeserving, it would be odd to place limits on the scope of that justice, those places at the banqueting table. When Jesus speaks of his death in the Gospel of John, he offers these words: "'Now is the judgment of this world; now the ruler of this world will be driven out. And I, when I am lifted up from the earth, will draw all people to myself'" (John 12:31–32). It is not our task to place limits on the Last Judgment; it is not our place to specify who is in and who is out. The far horizon of hope in Christ's return necessarily entails hope for the whole world, no exceptions. Christ is the One who draws all people to himself.

Christians, then, need not panic over their status or the status of anyone else in relation to God's judgment and the promise of the messianic banquet. Rather, we live out of thanks for God's grace given in Christ. We ask the wrong question if we ask, "Who's in, and who's out?" Belief in Christ's return and the Last Judgment does not boil down to the separation of the saved from the damned but indicates the certain establishment of God's justice, represented in a banquet where all are invited, no exceptions. That is more than enough to sustain hope.

QUESTIONS FOR DISCUSSION

1. What are your experiences of judgment or of being judged, and how are they different from an understanding of Jesus Christ as the final judge?
2. What does the example of Jesus Christ show us about the relationship between justice and mercy?
3. Why have Christians so often focused on the time of Christ's return?

5

The New Creation

When we moved to Texas, our family grew: we inherited a cat by the name of Whitney. The previous owners of the house we bought told us that she was a stray who showed up on their front porch one day. And she stayed there. She stayed when the previous owners moved out, and she stayed when we arrived, so our family increased by one. We were not what many would call "cat people," but Whitney changed that for us. Eventually, she moved into the house, charming each of us in cuddles, purrs, and meows. We grew to love her as she slept at the foot of our bed and as she greeted us each morning. Whitney was happiest when we held her and stroked her mottled fur.

We didn't know how old Whitney was, but after several years it became clear that she was reaching old age. The last months of her life were not her best, but she still loved to be held, still loved to be touched. After Whitney died, we held an impromptu memorial service: each of us remembered her with words, said a prayer, and cried. Then our daughter Grace asked, "Is Whitney in heaven?"

The answer to Grace's relatively simple question has not been uniform throughout Christian history. In many generations of the church, theologians would have answered "No" on the grounds that animals are not created in God's image and therefore not fitted for communion with God. How do we understand the end of creation as it relates to the nonhuman world? Thus far, this exploration of Christian hope has focused on its personal and social dimensions, which is where many treatments of Christian hope end. But there is something more—hope's cosmic dimension—though that dimension has become more difficult to uncover in light of modern preoccupations with the individual.

In the present day, much popular Christianity has become increasingly indi-vidualistic. The oft-heard query "Are you saved?" turns the focus of Christian hope squarely on oneself. A well-meaning teacher in a Sunday school class of my youth once posed a question to us: "What is the most important event in the universe?" Several of us upstart theologians hazarded various guesses. "Creation," one of us said. "The birth of Jesus," another quipped. "The resur-rection," chimed in yet a third student. None of us, to our chagrin, was right in the eyes of that teacher. Finally, after he had stumped us, he told us the real answer: "The most important event in the universe is when you accept Jesus Christ as your personal Lord and Savior; without doing that, all these other things don't mean a thing." We were moved by these comments so much that we could hardly speak. His answer indicated that the cosmic promises of Christian faith are also intensely personal: God makes these promises to each one of us.

The fact that I remember this incident some twenty-five years later under-scores the impact this teacher's statement made on me. Yet something about his statement is perplexing and even contradictory to the broad themes of Christian hope as I've come to understand them in subsequent years. It makes the most important subject in Christian faith *myself*—so important, in fact, that my faith became the most important event in the universe—more impor-tant than a community, more important than creation, more important than grace. I doubt it was my teacher's intent that day to place ourselves at the center of all things. He probably was just trying to prick our youthful piety a bit. But his rhetoric is one example of how Christian hope has become more and more individualistic in the present age, whether we encounter it in a fire-and-brimstone tractate from a local Bible church, in the commercial appeal of a televangelist, or the lesson plans of a well-meaning Sunday school teacher. Too often in the present age the question of Christian hope has become "What will happen to *me*?"

The Reformed faith, by contrast, understands Christian hope not chiefly as a personal event but as a communal and cosmic vision: embracing, sustain-ing, and re-creating all that God has made. Our faith, as we will discover in this chapter, stresses a God who makes *all things* new, who promises a new creation that encompasses far more than "righteous" individuals. In Christ, plants and persons, rocks and rivers, deer and snakes, planets and stars are redeemed by grace. This is a story that takes us out of the center. In order to take a first glimpse at it, we will look at some distortions of cosmic hope before turning to the biblical theme of re-creation, culminating in a city that God renews.

THE DESTRUCTION OF CREATION?

We have already seen in chapter 3 how Gnosticism vied with Christianity over how to value—or not value—the human body. Whereas the Gnostics disparaged the body, pointing to the need for the divine spark within us to escape its fleshy confines, orthodox Christianity emphasized the resurrection of the body, affirming its essential value and goodness. For the Gnostics, the created world was also a prison, bound as it was to sin. The created order, as glimpsed through Gnostic eyes, had little hope. Only the annihilation of all physical things could free us for spiritual relation with God. The worldview of the Gnostics, in other words, was intensely dualistic. Hope, goodness, and truth could be found only in purely "spiritual" things that were untainted by bodily and earthly pollution. The Gnostics did not merely distinguish the earthly from the spiritual; their vision of hope keeps them eternally apart. At the end of time, only the spiritual endures as it casts off the shackles of body and earth.

Though this message may have appealed to some of the early Christians who experienced the horrors of persecution (and perhaps even influenced some of the writers of the New Testament, such as 1 John with its strong polarities of light and darkness), the orthodox consensus argued vociferously against it. How could a faith that affirms the goodness of creation abandon creation to destruction at the end of time? The early Christians looked to the first chapter of Genesis, which offers seven distinct affirmations of created goodness: on successive days of creation, God beholds what God has made and pronounces it "good," culminating in the final day of creation, where God sees everything and claims it "very good." The early Christian consensus rejected Gnosticism because it suggested an arbitrary God who creates in goodness, covenants with Israel, and gives grace to the world in Christ only to withhold grace and destroy the good things that God has made in the end. What God destroys, according to the consensus, is not the body or creation but the forces of evil, sin, and death. Though apocalyptic literature within the Bible does at times rely on the language of destruction, this destruction is not for the earth but for the powers that threaten the earth's life. The book of Revelation is fascinating in this regard, as it depicts powers of greed and violence that are ultimately brought to nothing by God's grace and power:

> "The nations raged,
>   but your wrath has come,
>   and the time for judging the dead,
> for rewarding your servants, the prophets

and saints and all who fear your name,
    both small and great,
and for destroying those who destroy the earth."
                                    Rev. 11:18

What is destroyed in Revelation, in other words, are the forces of destruction that work against God's purposes and twist blessing into curse, life into death.

Throughout the book, these forces are portrayed with vivid images of beasts, whores, and dragons. One temptation throughout the ages has been to identify particular persons with these mythical figures. But to do so invariably is to place these characters on center stage, something the author of Revelation does not do. The point of these images, in the end, is to show how their presence and rule are ephemeral and ultimately empty. Threatening as they may appear, they stand only as a parody of God's eternity. Later in the book, the author describes the imminent demise of the beast, using language that stands in direct contrast to the God who is and was and is to come (1:4). "'The beast that you saw was, and is not, and is about to ascend from the bottomless pit and go to destruction'" (17:8a). Gnosticism veers toward polytheism, suggesting a good god who reigns over the spiritual realm and an evil being who holds sway among flesh and blood. Where Christianity differs is in its unwavering insistence on God's sovereignty: God is a God of all creation, not merely a God of one aspect of creation deemed more spiritual than another.

Imagery of destruction appears rather infrequently throughout Scripture. Those things destined for destruction, moreover, are revealed as nothing in light of God's grace in Jesus Christ. The powers of evil, sin, and death are not independent forces over and against God; instead, they represent the futility of living apart from God. Second Thessalonians holds that even the lawless one, "apparent in the working of Satan" (2 Thess. 2:9) comes to nothing: "And then the lawless one will be revealed, whom the Lord Jesus will destroy with the breath of his mouth, annihilating him by the manifestation of his coming" (2 Thess. 2:8). As sin, death, and evil desperately grasp for power, they self-destruct and are overcome by the grace of Christ. Christian apocalypticism displays the cosmic dimension of hope for all to see. In its sweeping, parabolic imagery, God redeems and transforms not simply human beings but the entire created order. Here powers, creatures, beasts, and rivers are reoriented by God's grace. What is graced with life grows into new life while what turns from grace is revealed as nothing. Even amid the imagery of battle (which we will explore in chapter 8), what holds the final word is not destruction but God's promise of a new creation.

Despite the early church's attempts to reject it, Gnosticism abides in the contemporary church. Some of its continued influence is evident in our tendencies to understand the spirit apart from the body and in an increasing sense of resignation in the face of calamities that face the planet. Some Christians retreat from the monumental injustices of our time—racial, economic, and ecological—taking heart that our efforts for justice make little difference, for God will destroy evil and fix everything in the end. The planet, according to this view, is going to hell in a handbasket, and we might as well wait for divine intervention to mend the mess. Former U.S. Secretary of the Interior James Watt, an apocalyptic Christian, was reported to have been unconcerned about our accelerating consumption of natural resources and environmental pollution because the end of the world was at hand; his beliefs, accordingly, abetted some of the most substantial rollbacks of environmental laws in U.S. history. Sometimes, a distorted sense of Christian hope can not only foster "do-nothingism" but also lead to willful disregard of God's creation. In the meantime, we live in the wake of this resignation. As global temperatures continue to rise, as potable water becomes scarcer in all regions of the globe, as species disappear at alarming rates, we must ask ourselves, Do our beliefs about the end times stress our dependence on an earth that God pronounces as "very good," or do they encourage us to use the earth as a disposable commodity, fostering the destruction that Scripture so loudly laments?

New forms of Christian Gnosticism have doubtless contributed to the current environmental mess, but so too have excessively personal readings of the Gospel. When we consider our salvation to be the "most important event in the universe," we are liable to see everything else in light of ourselves. Creation then becomes our possession rather than God's. A proper understanding of our place in the world, however, takes us out of the center. As contemporary Reformed theologian Jürgen Moltmann writes, "Interpreting the world as God's creation means precisely *not* viewing it as the world of human beings, and taking possession of it accordingly."[1] What is to keep Christians from reducing creation to resources for our own exploitation? Recalling that the world is very good and that the first task given to humanity in the Genesis narrative is to till the garden and keep it (Gen. 2:15)—work that underscores our dependence on the earth—encourages us to be mindful of the fruitfulness and well-being of all living things. Whatever we claim about the end times must also hearken the words uttered at the beginning of time.

A bumper sticker popular several years ago captured the resignation of a weary age: "Beam me up, Scotty; this planet sucks!" Though this proclamation, for now, has disappeared from public view, the attitude behind it remains. Much news about global warming, for example, seems focused on how to live with climate change instead of curbing habits that might ameliorate the problem. In the coming years, we will surely hear frequent advice to seek higher ground as oceans rise and to plan for new agricultural regions that will emerge as old ones become deserts. Whether we long to escape from a planet that "sucks" or resign ourselves to live in an increasingly inhospitable one, these messages from bumper stickers and the mass media suggest that planetary life is a burden.

The cosmic reach of Christian hope, however, presents an alternative vision. Creaturely life on this planet is not a burden but a blessing. Christ comes to redeem creation, not to teleport us out of it. He comes not so we might be relieved of misery and placed somewhere else but so that we might have life and have it abundantly (John 10:10), right here, right now, and into God's future. In the midst of all that threatens life, whether ecological poison, economic oppression, physical violence, or the scourge of sexism and racism, our glance to the future is not resignation but hope. God promises a new creation, which is the renewal—not the destruction—of everything God has made.

"SEE, I AM MAKING ALL THINGS NEW"

Near the conclusion to the book of Revelation, the author has a vision of the new heaven and earth as the new Jerusalem descends from heaven, "prepared as a bride adorned for her husband" (21:2). As this dazzling sight appears, a voice from the throne proclaims that God's home is "'among mortals,'" not apart from the earth in celestial isolation. Adding to the splendor, the voice resounds, "'See, I am making all things new'" (Rev. 21:3–5). Here the cosmic breadth of Christian hope is on full display. How are we to understand this vision? As design plans for the new creation, much like an architect's blueprint? Hardly. The book of Revelation expresses in human images and phrases what is ultimately inexpressible: the shape of the world's life as it grows into and from the life of God. John Calvin described Scripture as God's lisp to us, God's condescension to us using *our words*, knowing full well that they cannot express everything about God or the future God has in store for us. We should read the book of Revelation—and all Scripture—in the ways that Calvin suggested: not as a blueprint for the future but as a true expression of hope that encompasses the whole world. Sometimes in our history as church we have missed the forest (the vision of hope for the world) by fixating on one particular tree (Who is the beast? Will the new Jerusalem look *exactly* like the vision we have in Rev. 21?).

To place hope in the God who redeems all things in Jesus Christ and promises a day in which death will be no more is to recognize that our own well-being is bound up with the well-being of the cosmos. Christians grieve for the world as they hope for the world. The apostle Paul is strikingly realistic as he describes creation's longing for fulfillment:

> Creation itself will be set free from its bondage to decay and will obtain the freedom of the glory of the children of God. We know that the whole creation has been groaning in labor pains until now; and not only the creation, but we ourselves, who have the first fruits of the Spirit, groan inwardly while we wait for adoption, the redemption of our bodies. (Rom. 8:21–23)

Paul's vision is cosmic: salvation is not simply for human beings but for all creation. In the present, nature bears traces of the violence that infects human life; decay seems to hold the final word. This is not a starry-eyed optimism that simply accepts things as they are; it longs for change, transformation, and the coming of God's kingdom. In the nearly two thousand years since Paul penned this letter, his vision of creation's "groaning" has only become more apparent. As waterways become clogged with waste and increasingly devoid of aquatic life, we hear the groaning of creation. As factories in Asia and cars in the United States foul air that all persons across the globe breathe, we recognize that this groaning is the result of our own endeavors. Nature needs redemption not because of some flaw within itself but because of the damage human beings inflict on it. Misguided by our own attempts at mastery over nature, we are only now awakening to the horrors of our own making. We do not need to look to the book of Revelation to sense the scope of cosmic catastrophe; we need only walk out our front door.

A Christian does not wear rose-tinted glasses but remains hopeful because human violence and greed do not hold the final word. The good news is that in Christ and through the Spirit, we are taken into God's abundant life and become participants in the life given for the world. Christian hope doesn't mean that we sit passively for Christ to come; instead, we recognize that he frees us from the prison of violence and releases our lives in the service of all life. Labors that address the groaning of creation—be they legislative efforts that address global warming, backyard gardening, or carpooling—are small responses to the life God gives to the world. They do not hasten the kingdom's coming, but they share in the promise of abundant life for all, hearkening the fulfillment of creation in God's very life.

The renewal of heaven and earth in Jesus Christ is both a last thing promised at the end of time and a first thing written into the fabric of creation. As the author of Colossians writes,

> He is the image of the invisible God, the firstborn of all creation; for in him all things in heaven and on earth were created, things visible

and invisible . . . and through him God was pleased to reconcile to himself all things, whether on earth or in heaven, by making peace through the blood of his cross. (Col. 1:15–16, 20)

Christian hope for the fulfillment of creation is retrospective and prospective: the one in whom all things are created is also the end of all things. We and all that is—plants, rocks, mountains, trees, plankton, and whales—come from Christ and to Christ we return.

The redemption of all creation in and through Christ, then, is more than a cosmic repair job. God does not send Christ to the world as a bandage for sin and response to human waywardness; rather, God comes in Christ to communicate the fullness of God's very self, so that all might have life through him. God does not redeem one aspect of life to the exclusion of others. As the Confession of 1967 states,

> God's redeeming work in Jesus Christ embraces the whole of man's life: social and cultural, economic and political, scientific and technological, individual and corporate. It includes man's natural environment as exploited and despoiled by sin. It is the will of God that his purpose for human life shall be fulfilled under the rule of Christ and all evil be banished from his creation. (9.53)

God's desire is for eternal relationship with creation as God embraces creation in the flesh. The end of all things is, in this sense, a homecoming as well. As God makes all things new, we are brought to where we were meant to be all along. As the prologue to John's Gospel echoes, "All things came into being through him, and without him not one thing came into being. What has come into being in him was life, and the life was the light of all people" (John 1:3–4). God's extension of life to all things continues unabated, forever and ever.

Lest we think that this promise of fulfillment is extended only to human persons, the imagery from the prophets—who announce the coming of the Day of the Lord—encompasses all creatures. For Isaiah, the present violence that infects creation is transformed on that day, gathering all animals in a peaceable kingdom:

> The wolf and the lamb shall feed together,
>   the lion shall eat straw like the ox;
> but the serpent—its food shall be dust!
> They shall not hurt or destroy on all my holy mountain.
>   Isa. 65:25

Human persons, too, are put in their place, not as lords who wield power over creation but as creatures who live with and for other creatures:

The nursing child shall play over the hole of the asp,
    and the weaned child shall put its hand on the adder's den.
They will not hurt or destroy
    on all my holy mountain;
for the earth will be full of the knowledge of the Lord
    as the waters cover the sea.
                                                    Isa. 11:8–9

In the arresting image of a child playing near a snake—a situation that would likely lead to death in the present age—Isaiah makes clear the existence of all creatures for one another and the destiny of all creatures in God's very life.

We are now in a better position to respond to Grace's question that began this chapter: Yes, God desires communion with all of creation. Life is given in Christ, not selectively to a few rational beings, but indiscriminately and abundantly to all. If heaven represents the enduring character of relationship with God, which no attempt of ours can obstruct, then, yes, Whitney is in heaven, experiencing the abundant life given to the universe. And so, too, are all God's creatures.

A CITY AND A RIVER

In popular imagination, the blessedness of eternal communion with God often connotes rest for the weary. Cartoons and movies depict heaven as a scene of pastoral bliss, complete with naps and endless lollygagging. The new creation represents a return to Eden devoid of the command to tend the garden and keep it, a place far from the chaos of urban life where we can finally rest in peace. If other creatures appear at all, they serve as a backdrop to our human leisure. In some versions of this ultimately happy ending, other creatures (and even nature itself) hardly appear. Instead, we catch a glimpse of human beings living in the light of God, reposing on clouds, perhaps strumming a harp, but certainly pursuing no other work save these few heavenly chords. It is surprising that these images have such staying power in the popular imagination, for nowhere in Scripture does anything like them occur. Instead of depicting the new creation as an escape from creation or seeing nature as a backdrop for human bliss, biblical traditions display a surprising interaction between the so-called natural world and the work of human hands.

The new creation as represented in Scripture is not a return to Eden. The Bible, after all, begins in a garden and ends in a city. What are we to make of this? Revelation 21–22 provides a sustained exposition of eternal blessedness. In it, a city descends from heaven, brightly adorned as if for a wedding. And in great detail, the narrator of this vision describes each adornment and feature, among which is the absence of a temple. In this new city, there will be no need for a temple, because the temple will be the Lord God the Almighty. One might suspect cities to disappear in the new creation since they represent the work of human hands, which falls far short of God's intent. In the present age, cities epitomize the injustice and violence of life on planet earth. In them we behold the massive gulf between rich and poor, as the poor are concentrated in ghettos of limited opportunity, far from places of commerce, and the rich ensconce themselves in gated, exclusive communities. In cities, we witness the violence bred by limited economic opportunity and easy access to guns. In cities we encounter ravaging diseases like AIDS and breathe air fouled by smokestacks and tailpipes. In cities, racial segregation manifests itself anew, even after decades of struggle against it. The new creation is found in a city? Of all things!

But God redeems the work of human hands that has created injustice and oppression. In this new city, people "bring into it the glory and the honor of the nations" (Rev. 21:26). In this city, all peoples are welcome; in this city, gates are always open; in this city, there is no darkness; in this city all participate in abundance as God's glory is revealed for all. Cities built by human beings become God's dwelling place in the new creation, a dwelling place so intimate that there is no longer any need for a temple. Unlike the cities of our day, moreover, where work and the fruits of labor are hoarded and some cannot find work, the work of this city is shared. Here, the glory of *all* nations is brought together.

But this imagery of a city suggests something more. Here we encounter not simply the redemption of human work but the merging of our work with the bounty of creation. The vision of this new Jerusalem depicts a confluence of a renewed city with the bounty of creation:

> Then the angel showed me the river of the water of life, bright as crystal, flowing from the throne of God and of the Lamb through the middle of the street of the city. On either side of the river is the tree of life with its twelve kinds of fruit, producing its fruit each month; and the leaves of the tree are for the healing of the nations. (Rev. 22:1–2)

Here a river that has been polluted flows crystal clear, watering the land and nourishing the trees that present their fruits for all. A garden appears in the midst of the city. The new creation does not erase what human beings have done; nor does it elevate humans above all else in creation. Instead, we glimpse a harmonious whole, a city that thrives in the bounty of creation and nature renewed by the hand of God. In the end, nothing is lost: no bird, rock, or river is left behind or destroyed. All is renewed by and through God's grace. The city and the garden coexist, and in them is life for the world.

QUESTIONS FOR DISCUSSION

1. Why is it important for Christians to include nonhuman creation in our vision of Christian hope?
2. The Bible begins in a garden and ends in a city. What significance does this beginning and ending have for Christian hope?
3. How does our understanding of creation affect our care for the natural world?

PART III

Contested Questions

Armageddon, the antichrist, the rapture, heaven and hell: These images proliferate in many contemporary discussions about the end of the world. Proclaimed loudly by street-corner evangelists, they often seem bewildering to mainline Protestants and Catholics, perhaps even embarrassing. We turn now to some of the more controversial themes of Christian hope. How does the vision of hope outlined in the previous section come to grips with the more sensational figures and events that claim to mark the end of time? By addressing themes that the mainline churches often avoid, we find surprising resources as we debunk some prominent myths.

6

What about the Rapture?

LEFT BEHIND?

"Passengers aboard a Boeing 747 en route to Europe disappear. Instantly, nothing remains except their rumpled piles of clothes, jewelry, fillings, surgical pins, and the like. All over the world in a flash, cars are left unmanned. Terror and chaos continues worldwide as the cataclysm unfolds. For those left behind, the apocalypse has just begun."[1] So reads a preview of *Left Behind*,[2] one of the best-selling books in the history of publishing, a book that Jerry Falwell has claimed to be unequaled in its impact on American Christianity, except for the Bible. The book is the first of a twelve-volume series of "Christian fiction" (and an additional three prequels and one epilogue), written by Tim LaHaye and Jerry Jenkins, that boasts a combined sales of more than 65 million copies. In this advertising blurb, readers encounter a description of the "rapture," the inaugurating event of the end times, in which the righteous, who are still living when Christ comes again, are lifted from earth to gather with Christ in the heavens before tribulations rage, signaling the final battle between God and Satan. The premise for this entire novel comes from one verse in Paul's first letter to the Thessalonians: "Then we who are alive, who are left, will be caught up in the clouds together with them to meet the Lord in the air; and so we will be with the Lord forever" (1 Thess. 4:17). Since the stunning success of the Left Behind series has spawned much conversation about the "rapture" (a term that does *not* appear in Scripture), we must consider its purportedly biblical roots. The books, after all, have become popular not only in fundamentalist circles but in Presbyterian, Lutheran, Methodist, and Catholic contexts as well.

Knowing something about the authors helps us understand the theology behind the book series (which now includes movies as well). LaHaye, longtime pastor of a fundamentalist-apocalyptic church in San Diego, has authored more than fifty books on a wide variety of topics. Founder of San Diego Christian College, LaHaye no longer serves as pastor of a church and has devoted his recent ministry to writing and speaking. His theological education includes a bachelor's degree from Bob Jones University, though that education does not include the advanced studies typically required for seminary and university professors. Over the years, LaHaye's ministry has generated significant controversy. He has claimed that Roman Catholicism is "pseudo-Christian"; has devoted substantial energy toward combating what he considers the vileness of homosexuality; and has claimed that a shadowy, secretive group known as the "Illuminati" has gained control over world affairs, engineering takeovers of universities, the United Nations, mass media, and other organizations, such as the NAACP, NOW, and Planned Parenthood. These conspirators, LaHaye claims, are bent on destroying Christianity and its values. Jenkins, by contrast, does not have advanced degrees in theology and has made his living as a cartoonist and novelist, mainly in the areas of religious fiction but also in sports biography. His written work, comprising more than 150 books, has generated significantly less public controversy.

Though the authors acknowledge the Left Behind series as works of fiction, they stand firmly behind the belief in a literal rapture that will remove the righteous from jet planes, automobiles, and whatever other situations persons find themselves in when Christ returns. The cosmic battle between Satan and the armies of Christ, moreover, is real and will take place in the Middle East. Both authors have indicated that these historical events will happen sooner rather than later. The official Web site for the Left Behind series makes the following claims: "More prophecies were likely fulfilled in 1948 when Israel became an Independent nation and in 1967 when Israel regained control of Jerusalem from Jordan in the Six Day War. . . . As incredible as the Rapture, the Antichrist, the Tribulation, the mark of the beast, and the Millennium sound, they really are going to happen because the Bible says they will!"[3]

LaHaye and Jenkins, broadly speaking, stand within a wing of Christianity known as apocalyptic dispensationalism, as indicated by their fervent belief in an imminent end of the age, prefigured by discrete *dispensations* that mark God's covenant with humanity, human unfaithfulness, and the rise and fall of earthly powers. According to most dispensationalists, we now live in the sixth of seven dispensations, which will end with tribulation, a final battle of good and evil, and God's victory over all earthly powers, ushering in a thousand-year reign of Christ. Though similar theologies have emerged occasionally within the church (typically among dissenting groups that conceived the established churches as a threat to genuine faith), only in the last 150 years has dispensationalism emerged in a loud voice, and with distinctively American emphases. The idea of being "left behind," then, is a relatively recent development in Christian eschatology. For the vast span of the church's history, neither the periodization of history into "dispensations" nor the "rapture" has figured prominently in Christian teaching about the last things.

LaHaye and Jenkins take one verse of Scripture and develop a novel from it. By contrast, Calvin, like the Reformers of his day, cites 1 Thess. 4:17 sparingly in his *Institutes* and considers it to be a sign that all persons, living and dead, are summoned before Christ as judge and savior (2.16.17). For him, the supposed "rapture" is less about a description of what happens to the living when Christ comes again and more a statement about the One we belong to in life and death. How can a Reformed understanding of hope grapple with the theology presented in *Left Behind*? If Reformed Christianity is to offer an alternative to dispensationalism, we ought to read Paul's letter to the Thessalonians carefully.

REREADING 1 THESSALONIANS

Most New Testament scholars consider 1 Thessalonians to be Paul's earliest extant letter, perhaps the earliest piece of the New Testament itself. When we read it, we glimpse Christianity in its earliest stages of development. First Thessalonians gets close to our roots as a church.

Three prominent themes emerge in this comparatively brief letter: (1) Paul's expectation of the imminent return of Christ as Lord; (2) guidelines for living in community in light of his return; and (3) Paul's response to controversy regarding those who have died in the church prior to Christ's return. Unlike some of Paul's other letters that combat false teachings, 1 Thessalonians serves chiefly as encouragement and exhortation. Paul's praise of the Thessalonians in 1:6–8 is nearly unprecedented, noting how they "became an example to all the believers in Macedonia and Achaia. For the word of the Lord has sounded forth from you not only in Macedonia and Achaia, but in every place your faith in God has become known, so that we have no need to speak about it" (vv. 7–8). Paul writes knowing the strength of the community, further edifying and encouraging them in light of Christ's coming. He means not to persuade or to scold them into living differently, but to strengthen them in what they are already doing.

Paul considers his labors as evangelist and the Thessalonians' labors for the kingdom against a vast, cosmic backdrop. The struggle between God and Satan is, in some sense, the work that matters in history. Paul interprets his own inability to return to Thessalonica in light of that struggle: "For we wanted to come to you—certainly I, Paul, wanted to again and again—but Satan blocked our way" (2:18). Paul's own work as missionary to the Gentiles and the Thessalonians' labors for the kingdom fit into a story that has decisive significance for the life of the world.

In light of Christ's imminent return and the life-and-death struggles of the cosmos, how are believers to live? For Paul, the answer to that question is found neither in passive waiting for the Lord nor unrestrained licentiousness. Christians do not eat and drink as usual, for tomorrow they die; rather, the Lord's coming provides impetus for restraining the body. Paul warns against *porneia* (4:3), a term that is difficult to translate but is variously translated as "fornication" or "sexual immorality." The control of the sexual body, in light of Christ's coming, is a mark of "holiness and honor" in contrast to "the Gentiles who do not know God" (4:4–5). Paul exhorts the believers, moreover, "to aspire to live quietly, to mind [their] own affairs, and to work with [their] hands" (4:11), an appeal to the self-sufficiency of the group as it is marked out from the dominant Greco-Roman culture. The overarching command for the group, however, is to increase in love: the injunctions to work, restrain sexual passion, and live quietly occur with the intent of loving one another "more and more" (4:10). The life of the body—those gathered in Christ's name who await his coming—makes a difference, and believers ought to live in ways that reflect Christ's lordship of the body.

The fateful verses that have sometimes been construed as "rapture" occur in this context of Paul's encouragement to the Thessalonians. Paul writes in response to some controversy over the status of those in the community who have died before Christ's return. Would the departed, too, participate in the glory of Christ's return? In this section, the reader observes Paul's imminent sense of Christ's return and his pastoral intent of reassuring the congregation that the living *and* the dead will be blessed by Christ's coming: "We do not want you to be uninformed, brothers and sisters, about those who have died, so that you may not grieve as others do who have no hope. For since we believe that Jesus died and rose again, even so, through Jesus, God will bring with him those who have died" (4:13–14). In Paul's eyes, the dead in Christ "will rise first" (4:16). Then, the famous verses: "Then we who are alive, who are left, will be caught up in the clouds together with them to meet the Lord in the air; and so we will be with the Lord forever. Therefore encourage one another with these words" (4:17–18). Paul's last sentence here is critical: this message is for encouragement, to reassure the Thessalonians that, living or dead, all who are in Christ will participate in the glory of his coming. If we read the entire letter, it becomes clear that Paul is not chiefly concerned with chronologies and predictions about the mode of Christ's coming, but with reassuring the community that all will participate in that blessedness. Their conduct as a church, accordingly, ought to reflect that hope.

The letter's conclusion reinforces that aim, as Paul states, "Whether we are awake or asleep we may live with him. Therefore encourage one another and build up each other, as indeed you are doing" (5:10–11). Paul then closes with a host of further injunctions for the sustained life of the community: honoring leadership roles, laboring for peace, helping the weak, encouraging the faint-hearted, refusing to render evil for evil, rejoicing, praying, and giving thanks (5:12–18). His point is not to predict the exact nature of Christ's return but to sustain the life of the community in light of Christ's return. An echo of this sentiment is contained in the Brief Statement of Faith, which begins, "In life and in death we belong to God" (10.1). Paul sustains that hope, more than any other, in his earliest letter.

ROADMAP OF FUTURE EVENTS OR IMAGES OF HOPE?

LaHaye and Jenkins consider 1 Thessalonians as a road map for the future. In their interpretation, Paul offers literal descriptions of events yet to come, where we should expect trumpets, an archangel, and a gathering of the living in the air, exactly as those few verses seem to depict them. But if Paul is offering a road map, then consider this: The map, if we are to take it at face value, was wrong. Why? Because Paul clearly expected the return of Christ to happen within his lifetime. Paul would not be writing to a congregation explaining what would happen to the living if he did not expect some—if not most—of the Thessalonians to be living at the time of Christ's return. Paul, like the vast majority of Christians in that first generation of the church, expected Christ to return very soon. But on this small detail, Paul and others were wrong. Does this stubborn fact, a fact that every generation in the church has had to wrestle with since then, render null and void the hope expressed in this letter and every other New Testament document? Only if we take these documents to be blueprints for future events that will unfold along literal lines, a way of reading Scripture that runs contrary to most of the church's history. For the bulk of that history, the Bible was not read as a fortune-telling book or a chronicle that outlined future events; rather, it was a book that sustained the faith, hope, and love of the community in light of God's coming in Jesus Christ by the power of the Holy Spirit by indicating what God is doing *now*. The Bible is the church's book, a book that sustains and guides the community in faith for the life of the world by opening our eyes to God's presence and grace. We ought to remember this especially when we come face-to-face with the more apocalyptic sections of the Bible. Their chief intent, then as well as now, is not to predict or outline future events but to sustain hope in light of present struggle.

It is odd that present-day dispensationalists, like LaHaye and Jenkins, ignore those parts of Paul's "road map" that have turned out to be wrong (i.e., that Christ would return within Paul's lifetime) and accept others as literal truths that point to the precise unfolding of Christ's coming. Only within the past 150 years have Christians made such intensive efforts to use the Bible as a guidebook for the future. Where earlier generations have rested in mystery, many in the present want to answer every question under the sun, right down to the details of what it will look like for those traveling on airliners when Christ returns. What has sustained the earliest generations of the church ought to be enough to sustain us: Christ has died, Christ is risen, Christ will come again. But for many dispensationalists, this just doesn't seem to be enough.

We should read 1 Thessalonians 4 not as a guidebook but as a statement of hope that grounds the life of the community, the Thessalonian church as well as our own. That seems to have been Paul's intent, and it ought to be enough. If that is the case, then we ought not confuse hope for the future with a road map for the future; we ought not feel that the job of each generation is to unravel all mystery in the details of coming events. If, in life and death, we belong to God, then, as Paul writes elsewhere in Romans, nothing can separate us from the love of Jesus Christ: "neither death, nor life, . . . nor anything else in all creation" (Rom. 8:38–39). When Paul speaks of meeting the Lord in the air, he marks to whom we belong and how we honor Christ.[4] As the Lord of all, he announces hope for the world.

ARGUING WITH THE TEXT:
TEXTS OF TROUBLE AND TERROR

If we read 1 Thessalonians as a testimony of hope, then it is also important that we attend to those aspects of the text that have been used historically as instruments against hope. Contained within this letter is one of the most problematic and difficult passages for contemporary Christian-Jewish relations. I thus quote the text with trepidation:

> For you, brothers and sisters, became imitators of the churches of God in Christ Jesus that are in Judea, for you suffered the same things from your own compatriots as they did from the Jews, who killed both the Lord Jesus and the prophets, and drove us out; they displease God and oppose everyone by hindering us from speaking to the Gentiles so that they may be saved. Thus they have constantly been filling up the measure of their sins: but God's wrath has overtaken them at last. (1 Thess. 2:14–16)

From this text, the church has drawn all sorts of detestable inferences: Jews are Christ-killers; they deserve God's punishment; God has revoked the covenant God established with Israel. History is replete with sermons and treatises that have invoked these very words and argued for proselytizing and outright persecution of Jews. The church has more often been an accomplice in anti-Jewish activity than a voice against it, a legacy that is due, in part, to texts such as this one. Scholars puzzle about this passage: some have argued that it represents the editorial hand of a later writer; others that it represents some of the frustration of early Jewish Christians who experienced difficulty in synagogues. Whatever their circumstances, the terror and the pain of these words remain within the canon that Christians claim as authoritative.

What does it mean to cite the Bible as authority, especially with passages such as this, to say nothing of those passages that enjoin women to stay silent and slaves to be submissive? Does it mean that every jot and tittle of Scripture is a literal Word of God? Reformed Christianity has held, in general, that the words of Scripture are human words to which God accommodates Godself. Calvin was fond of the image of God lisping through the words of Scripture. Just as a parent will accommodate his or her adult speech to the "language" of a baby and communicate using the coos and gurgles of baby talk, so, too, does God accommodate the divine Word to the human words of Scripture. Both words speak the truth: a parent coos to communicate love; God uses our words to reveal Godself. Yet one should never confuse baby talk with adult speech and never pretend that *everything* of Godself is always revealed in the human words of Scripture. The human words of Scripture, moreover, reflect the circumstances, assumptions, and controversies of the times in which they were written. The Confession of 1967 offers a reminder of this, and of how important it is to remember that fact in the work of interpretation:

> The Bible is to be interpreted in the light of its witness to God's work of reconciliation in Christ. The Scriptures, given under the guidance of the Holy Spirit, are nevertheless the words of men, conditioned by the language, thought forms, and literary fashions of the places and times at which they were written. They reflect views of life, history, and the cosmos which were then current. (9.29)

There are places in the fabric of the biblical canon, moreover, that may even serve as an obstacle to hope and the new life of reconciliation in Jesus Christ. Contained within Scripture, often because of the sins of the church, are texts of terror. It is hard to read 1 Thess. 2:14–16 and not be reminded of the church's own culpability in acts of terror against Jews. In light of that history, it is clear that this passage can be read in ways that work *against* hope. But if our guide is to interpret Scripture "in the light of its witness to God's work of reconciliation in Christ," then we stand in a better position to evaluate such texts.

How, then, are we to read them? Perhaps they stand as a negative witness against reconciliation in the broad witness of Scripture. Perhaps they stand as examples of the foibles and flaws of human language as an instrument of God's accommodation of God's Word. Perhaps they are examples of the petty human interests that are present in every human writer. But, whatever the case, we ought to acknowledge that sometimes our readings of Scripture need to be exorcised in the name of hope.[5] Accepting Scripture as authority means that the church is often called—in faithfulness to the authority of Christ—to argue with texts as well. To take a text seriously is not to follow it blindly in all cases but to wrestle with it.

Such wrestling, in the end, is an exercise in which LaHaye and Jenkins refuse to engage. Perhaps it is no surprise that Israel figures prominently at the outset of the Left Behind series, as the site of the final battles. Yet, in the end, the Jews become a foil to the truth revealed in Jesus Christ. The interest in Israel is a purely Christian interest; Jews come, in the end, to Christ. Thus the same old story is replayed: Jews are objects only fit for conversion. Here Christians tread a dangerous road again: potential anti-Jewish readings of Scripture are left unexamined, and the road map remains intact.

In reading our Scriptures, Christians can instead learn a lesson from our Jewish sisters and brothers as people of the book. Within Judaism is a long and rich tradition of midrash: of arguing with, wrestling with, and posing alternative readings of sacred texts. To live in faithfulness to a text and to the God who speaks through texts is to argue with it. For only in argument does one take it seriously enough to engage it as authority. Shouldn't we do the same with texts that have been cited as evidence of God's "rejection" of Israel? Of texts that have recently been assumed to outline the details of the future?

Paul does not focus primarily on "rapture" in 1 Thessalonians. His focus instead is on the present life of the community in light of its Lord and Savior, who promises to return. Hope lies not in the details of the mode and manner of his coming but in the conviction that he will come again to claim the living and the dead.

QUESTIONS FOR DISCUSSION

1. What is your reaction to dispensationalism? How do you respond to it? Why is it common among some Christians in the United States?
2. Can faithful Christians argue with Scripture?
3. How do 1 Thessalonians 4 and 5 sustain present hope? What is Paul's chief message in writing about Christ's coming?

7

What about Heaven and Hell?

POPULAR VISIONS OF HEAVEN AND HELL

Heaven is not our default destination. No one goes there automatically. Unless our sin problem is resolved, the only place we will go is our true default destination . . . Hell. . . . Throughout this book I will talk about being with Jesus in Heaven, being reunited with family and friends, and enjoying great adventures in Heaven. The great danger is that readers will assume they are headed for Heaven. Judging by what's said at most funerals, you'd think nearly everyone's going to Heaven, wouldn't you? But Jesus made it clear most people are not going to Heaven. . . . We dare not "wait and see" when it comes to what's on the other side of death. We shouldn't just cross our fingers and hope that our names are written in the Book of Life (Revelation 21:27). We can know, we should know, before we die. And because we may die at any time, we need to know now—not next month or next year. . . . It's of paramount importance to make sure you are going to Heaven, not Hell. The voice that whispers, "There's no hurry; put this book down; you can always think about it later," is not God's voice.[1]

These words were written by Randy Alcorn, a popular evangelist, in a Web posting titled, "Is Heaven Our Default Destination . . . Or Is Hell?" They reflect some popular, early twenty-first American assumptions about heaven, hell, and the afterlife. First is the fact that the question of where we are going, heaven or hell, is of "paramount importance" because it reflects the central concern of Christianity: our eternal destiny. Those who accept Christ are assured a place; those who reject him are damned for certain. Second, our eternal destiny is *our* responsibility: whether we wind up in heaven or hell depends on whether we have faith or not. We are, Alcorn urges, "to make sure" we are going to heaven, not hell. Finally, relatively few will make it to heaven, which makes it all the more imperative that we make sure our passports and boarding passes are in order. In Alcorn's understanding, heaven and hell are places that await us after death, though hell seems a far more spacious place, given its more numerous inhabitants. For Alcorn and many others, heaven is for those who exhibit faith while hell is for those without it. Devout Christians are destined for paradise while non-Christians (Mahatma Gandhi and the Dalai Lama included) will face eternal torment in hell.

One modification of this view is perhaps more common in contemporary American Christianity: heaven is a place for good people, regardless of religion or creed, while hell is a place for those who have committed unrepentantly evil acts. This schema appeals less to explicit Christian faith than it does to justice and our sense of goodness. If God is good and just, then God will account for the just and unjust actions that people commit during their lifetimes, rewarding those who work for justice, peace, and goodness and punishing those who dehumanize, commit senseless violence, and so on. In this understanding, Gandhi and the Dalai Lama also inherit eternal blessedness alongside St. Francis and Mother Teresa. Only those who commit evil acts solely for the sake of evil roast in the fires of hell: certainly Adolf Hitler and Jeffrey Dahmer, probably Josef Stalin and Judas Iscariot. The passport to either place, in this view, is whether one has done good, or mostly good, in one's life or not. This modified vision, however, shares in common with the first view the conviction that our eternal destiny remains our responsibility. We are the ones who punch our tickets to either destination.

What do Christians mean by "heaven" and "hell"? Are they places? Are they symbols for relationship or the absence of relationship with God? For some persons, the idea of heaven has proven an enticement to Christian faith. The ultimate payoff for having faith, in their view, is a life of eternal blessedness. For others, the very idea of hell provides the ultimate turnoff to Christianity. The idea of God's damning countless persons to eternal torments seems inconsistent with a God of love who seeks communion with all God's creatures. Why would God damn those whom God loves? Some have even claimed that the concept of hell bears much in common with child abuse: God is a Father who "loves" his children only to demonstrate that love by eternally punishing the rebellious ones. We wouldn't excuse such behavior for human parents who have run out of patience with a disobedient child, so why should we accept this behavior on God's part? Where is hope in that? When it comes to questions of heaven and hell, modern Christians are faced with a host of questions such as these.

REWARD AND PUNISHMENT?

One of the linchpins of Reformed Christianity is that human persons do not merit or earn salvation. Salvation, rather, comes to us freely through God's gift (grace alone), shown forth in our life by faith given to us in Jesus Christ (faith alone). By claiming that salvation was *by grace through faith*, the Reformers criticized abusive religious practices (such as selling indulgences so that buyers could earn salvation) and an overreliance on otherwise helpful religious practices pursued with the wrong intent (such as reciting a prescribed number of prayers or committing a specified number of good acts) to counteract accumulated sin. The problem with these practices was that it reduced salvation to something that humans earn through our actions—or salvation by works. In this scenario, human beings are helpless because we could *never* do enough to compensate for our sin. The slogans of "grace alone" and "faith alone," in this context, were enormously liberating, fostering trust in God rather than oneself. The good news of Christian faith was that our lives rested in the arms of an utterly gracious God.

In the present day, many understandings of faith resemble works all over again. Alcorn claims that we need to "make sure" we are going to heaven and have faith. Faith is what we believe, that is, whether we confess in our hearts Jesus Christ as Savior. Consistent with this understanding of faith is a prayer often found at the end of tractates: confessing sin, believing Jesus has died for our sins, and accepting him into our hearts. Notice how faith, thus construed, is something that we do for ourselves.

The Reformed confessions talk about faith differently: "Faith is a pure gift of God which God alone of his grace gives" (Second Helvetic Confession, 5.113). Or, again, faith is something that persons "have not of themselves; it is the gift of God" (Westminster, 6.068). In this view, we do not muster ourselves into faith or claim a belief as our own; rather, we accept a gift freely given. Faith, in the Reformed tradition, is a gift we receive from God rather than something we do.

One of the problems with popular understandings of heaven is that they often present heaven as an entitlement for the worthy. They make salvation and damnation the results of our work, all but eclipsing God's grace. But God's gifts are not gifts if they are deserved; God gives them to us for the sheer sake of giving. If the symbols of heaven and hell are to mean anything for us today, we need to strike the language of earning and deserving—however subtle it may be—from conversation.

Many popular understandings of heaven and hell assume that heaven is a reward for good behavior or faith and that hell is the punishment for bad behavior or lack of faith. But such understandings actually invert the Gospels' portrayals of salvation, where salvation comes not to the righteous but to those who know they are not righteous. As one who ate with tax collectors and sinners, Jesus often criticized those who claimed themselves to be good and righteous and sat at table with those whom good religious people should avoid. "'I have come to call not the righteous but sinners'" (Mark 2:17b). Jesus talks about salvation differently than do Alcorn and others in our time. Those few times Jesus utters the word "hell" is not in judging criminals, deviants, or unfaithful people but in castigating those who were most religious in his day. When he claims, rather harshly, "'You snakes, you brood of vipers! How can you escape being sentenced to hell?'" (Matt. 23:33), his audience is not a den of irreligious people but self-consciously religious folks, including some scribes and Pharisees. Heaven, for Jesus, is not the ultimate payoff for religion; rather, it's hell.

HELL: A BRIEF HISTORY

Jesus speaks of hell somewhat infrequently in the Gospels. Yet when he speaks of it, he reflects the Jewish assumptions of his time, assumptions that differ from earlier Old Testament understandings. If we could claim a biblical understanding of hell, we need to acknowledge the diversity of perspectives within the Bible itself. Hell, in the Scriptures, has a history.

The Old Testament seems to avoid hell entirely. Throughout the Pentateuch, Psalms, Wisdom literature, and Prophets an alternative image emerges: *Sheol*, a term that is hardly synonymous with later understandings of hell. Rather than a place for the wicked, Sheol is a symbol for the inescapability of death. The writer of Ecclesiastes notes, "Whatever your hand finds to do, do with your might; for there is no work or thought or knowledge or wisdom in Sheol, to which you are going" (Eccl. 9:10). As the home of the dead, Sheol does not stand outside God's presence and purposes. We need not fear death since Sheol itself lies within God's wisdom and guidance.

Even the most apocalyptic book of the Old Testament, Daniel, lacks the explicit imagery of hell that one might expect. The closest approach to hell occurs in Daniel's final chapter, which narrates an image of resurrection: "'Many of those who sleep in the dust of the earth shall awake, some to everlasting life, and some to shame and everlasting contempt'" (Dan. 12:2). For more extensive imagery of fire and brimstone, one looks to the Old Testament in vain. Clearly, the early Christian church developed its understanding of hell by looking elsewhere than to the Scriptures that Jesus held as authority.

Our word *hell* is a translation of the New Testament's *Gehenna*, a term referring to a valley south of Jerusalem that was associated with a pagan fire rite. The term names a place not in the next world but within the land of Israel, a place that became identified with religious practices that represented departures from Israel's faithfulness to God. Gradually, it seems, this place of other religious practices associated with fire took on eternal connotations, and these connotations occasionally find expression in some of Jesus' teachings.

When does Jesus invoke hell? The few times he does so are significant. One of them occurs in his radicalizing of the law, his more stringent application of the law to behavior:

> "You have heard that it was said to those of ancient times, 'You shall not murder'; and 'whoever murders shall be liable to judgment.' But I say to you that if you are angry with a brother or sister, you will be liable to judgment; and if you insult a brother or sister, you will be liable to the council; and if you say, 'You fool,' you will be liable to the hell of fire." (Matt. 5:21–22)

Jesus' words hardly mesh with today's popular conceptions of hell. Anger and calling someone else a fool makes one liable to hell? These seem rather petty offenses. But Jesus illustrates the breakdown of relationships that our words and actions breed: not just murder but anger, insult, and careless words. Hell, for Jesus, represents alienation between persons, whether brought about by insult or murder. When we rupture relationships among ourselves, we break relationship with God, experiencing hell in the midst of that brokenness.

At other places in Jesus' ministry, he invokes the image of "Hades," generally taken as a translation of the Hebrew *Sheol*. But here, the image conveys more freight than an Old Testament understanding of the realm of the dead. In his woes to unrepentant cities, Jesus inveighs,

> "And you, Capernaum,
>   will you be exalted to heaven?
>   No, you will be brought down to Hades.
> For if the deeds of power done in you had been done in Sodom, it would have remained until this day. But I tell you that on the day of judgment it will be more tolerable for the land of Sodom than for you." (Matt. 11:23–24)

Here Hades implies something more than death; it is a metaphor for a destiny that includes divine judgment. Beyond this, however, it's hard to say much. We don't know from the context *why* Jesus invokes woe on these cities other than their lack of repentance (Matt. 11:20). But if repentance includes the mending of relationships and restoration to community, then this teaching of Hades seems consistent with Jesus' earlier teaching of hell. Nonetheless, Jesus' own teachings are hardly the full-fledged images of hell that have become commonplace throughout the Christian church, from medieval frescoes to modern-day cartoons.

For the beginnings of such imagery, we have to turn to the book of Revelation. But there we find no mention of hell. Instead, we encounter a profusion of images, including "Hades," "the second death," and a lake of fire. Far from offering a seamless account of hell, Revelation presents a wealth of pictures that depict hell's fury as transient, occurring within God's saving purposes for the whole of creation. Most of these images occur toward the end of the book. In John's vision of the new heaven and the new earth, death, mourning, crying, and pain will end, while " 'the cowardly, the faithless, the polluted, the murderers, the fornicators, the sorcerers, the idolaters, and all liars, their place will be in the lake that burns with fire and sulfur, which is the second death' " (Rev. 21:7–8). In this vision, faithfulness until death truly makes a difference: in the face of persecution, one bears witness to the Lamb who was slain and belongs to him alone. The book of Revelation promises not solace to those who keep the faith but turmoil in the midst of an empire that wants to claim the Lamb's children as its own. Yet empire and its children will inherit the "second death." The contrasting images of a new creation and the lake of fire are testimony to a fundamental cosmic struggle, whether in John's day or our own: the struggle between life and death. In Christ, the slain Lamb, is life for the world; without him we reap death.

Revelation consistently denies the equality of the powers represented by these images. The powers of death, symbolized in the devil, the beast, and the false prophet, appear to reign for an instant but are destined for the lake of fire and eternal torment (20:7–10). So, too, are "Death and Hades" themselves (20:14). Yet, for all who share in the first resurrection, "the second death has no power" (20:6). In light of the God who gives life through Christ, even the powers of the devil and death are empty. For those who abide in Christ, there is nothing to fear, come hell or high water. Eternal torment, as imagined in Revelation, is not primarily for people, whether good or bad, but for powers that breed only death: the devil, the beast, and the false prophet. Revelation, then, provides less a blueprint for hell and more the hope that even when Death and Hades extend their reach on earth, they are destined to die. In light of God's saving grace, their power is empty.

THE DEVELOPMENT OF HEAVEN

Unlike hell, imagery of heaven appears abundantly throughout the Bible. But, like its infernal counterpart, heaven does not surface uniformly in the Scriptures. In the Old Testament, heaven refers most frequently not to God's dwelling place but to the skies, the heavens, which like the earth are the creation of God's hands. The God of Israel is the "maker of heaven and earth"

(Gen. 14:19). Generally speaking, when the Old Testament writers refer to God's presence in heaven, they do not exclude God's presence on earth. For God's dwelling place is also a tabernacle that Israel carries through the wilderness into the promised land, culminating in a temple that is God's home. Outsiders, such as Rahab the prostitute, may recognize God's presence most fully. Providing refuge to an advance team of Israelites before they settle the promised land, Rahab notes, "'The LORD your God is indeed God in heaven above and on earth below'" (Josh. 2:11).

Even the apocalyptic literature of the Old Testament does not portray heaven as a destination for the righteous but as the origin of the coming deliverer, whose reign will be everlasting, in contrast to Israel's temporary kingdoms:

> I saw one like a human being [Son of Man]
>   coming with the clouds of heaven. . . .
> To him was given dominion
>   and glory and kingship,
> that all peoples, nations, and languages
>   should serve him.
> His dominion is an everlasting dominion
>   that shall not pass away,
> and his kingship is one
>   that shall never be destroyed.
>   Dan. 7:13–14

Heaven is not a promised destiny for those who keep the covenant; heaven is the glory of God and the promise of God's eternal deliverance.

Common to both Testaments, however, is a three-tiered understanding of the cosmos. Earth lies at the center, with heaven above and an underworld below. When Jesus looked at the heavens, he, like Abraham, saw stars and sun revolving around the earth and likely imagined a realm of death below his feet. Such an understanding of the cosmos was hardly unique to the people Israel; it was common to most ancient cultures during this period of history. Only with Galileo's astronomical discoveries did this long-standing understanding of the cosmos begin to crumble, perhaps crumbling most slowly in the church, as evidenced in its heresy trial—and conviction—of Galileo. Considering this history, it is important to remember that, whatever they stand for, when the biblical authors wrote about heaven and hell, their understandings of the universe were different from our own.

In the New Testament, heaven emerges with slightly different emphases. Jesus speaks often about the kingdom of heaven, a symbol that stands for God's power and irrevocable promises. But Jesus also refers to heaven as compensation for the faithful during trying times, as he does in the Beatitudes:

> "Blessed are you when people revile you and persecute you and utter all kinds of evil against you falsely on my account. Rejoice and be glad, for your reward is great in heaven, for in the same way they persecuted the prophets who were before you." (Matt. 5:11–12)

Whether Jesus refers here to a place that one inhabits after death is open to question, since in other places in the Gospels he identifies the kingdom of heaven far more frequently with present acts and people, such as children:

> "Truly I tell you, unless you change and become like children, you will never enter the kingdom of heaven. Whoever becomes humble like this child is the greatest in the kingdom of heaven. Whoever welcomes one such child in my name welcomes me." (Matt. 18:2–5)

Inheritance of the kingdom of heaven, in this view, does not merely await us after death but occurs in the midst of earthly life.

In the letter to the Hebrews, heaven takes on different emphases. Here heaven represents not only the scope of divine majesty and power but a sanctuary that Jesus enters on behalf of the entire human species. Drawing on priestly imagery resonant with Israel's temple cult, Hebrews envisions Jesus entering heaven on our behalf, representing us to God and God to us: "For Christ did not enter a sanctuary made by human hands, a mere copy of the true one, but he entered into heaven itself, now to appear in the presence of God on our behalf" (Heb. 9:24). In this sustained meditation on Christ's atonement, heaven becomes the temple of temples, the place where the high priest, Christ, offers himself for the sin of the world. In Hebrews, heaven is a place: not a final destination for the righteous but the site of the universal sacrifice Jesus offers for the world. What happens on the cross, in this understanding, is not confined to earth but changes the course of heaven.

Does heaven ever appear as a destination for the faithful in the New Testament? Two narratives stand out as possibilities, one in the Gospels and another in Revelation. Let's look at each. The parable of the Rich Man and Lazarus, which occurs only in Luke (16:19–26), does not mention heaven, though it does refer to Hades. During his earthly life, the rich man refuses to acknowledge Lazarus, a poor man afflicted with sores, and fails to give Lazarus the scraps that fall from his table. When both men die, angels take Lazarus "'to be with Abraham'" (v. 22) while the rich man suffers torment in Hades. Details of the parable are suggestive and perplexing: the rich man sees Lazarus and appeals to Abraham for mercy, suggesting some kind of relationship and communication between the realms that each inhabit, though a chasm obstructs passage between them. The story, however, hardly presents a doctrine of heaven. Instead, it notes one of the stunning reversals that accompany Jesus' announcement of the kingdom, where the mighty are laid low and the lowly are exalted. Here is a vivid enactment of what Jesus has already proclaimed in the Beatitudes, enacted on a cosmic scale that transcends death. But the message that Jesus draws from this story is not to "believe and you will enter heaven," but rather to listen to Moses and the prophets (16:29). This parable draws our attention not simply to the afterlife but to the testimony that Israel has already received.

Finally, the book of Revelation contains abundant imagery of heaven, as the source of divine messengers, the abode of angels, and a place where many rejoice over the marriage of Christ the Lamb. Yet in Revelation the righteous do not rise to heaven; rather, heaven comes to earth in the new Jerusalem. Metaphors of descent rather than ascent predominate, culminating in an end where God comes to earth and makes a home "among mortals" (Rev. 21:3) in a city that offers light to the world. The righteous, in John's vision, do not "get into heaven" as much as heaven comes to them, in a renewal of earth and sky that has profound ecological implications (as we saw in chapter 5). In Revelation, heaven is not a destination that we gain admission to by faith (or works) but a promise given to all creation that God will make a home among us.

REFORMED CONFESSIONS: HEAVEN AND HELL AS FUTURE PRESENT

Between its New Testament foundations and the Middle Ages, the church began to represent heaven and hell as eternal destinations for the faithful and the wicked. Frescoes painted in countless churches throughout Europe reflect this development. In an age when few could read and write, artistic representations of the torments of hell and the blessedness of heaven offered vivid contrasts of the life-giving gospel amid death-dealing faithlessness and abandonment of God. Their artwork symbolized God's gift of grace and our turning from grace, with its eternal consequences. Heaven and hell became places populated by saints and sinners. Most Reformed confessions reflect this heritage. Westminster, for example, describes heaven and hell as places of blessing and torment:

> Then shall the righteous go into everlasting life, and receive the full-ness of joy and refreshing which shall come from the presence of the Lord: but the wicked, who know not God, and obey not the gospel of Jesus Christ, shall be cast into eternal torments, and punished with everlasting destruction from the presence of the Lord, and from the glory of his power. (6.181)

Yet Westminster also brings heaven to earth in commenting on the Lord's Prayer. To pray for God's will to be done "on earth as it is in heaven" is not to wait for a reward in heaven but to pray that "God, by his grace, would make us able and willing to know, obey, and submit to his will in all things, as the angels do in heaven" (7.103). Heaven in the early Reformed tradition is not simply a destination but a symbol for God's will on earth and our participation in that will by grace.

Another Reformation-era confession stresses how the reality of heaven and hell impinge on the life of this world. In its commentary on the Apostles' Creed, the Heidelberg Catechism meditates on Christ's descent into hell. This descent into the realm of the dead is significant not because it protects us in the afterlife but because it offers hope as we face suffering in this life. "In my severest tribulations I may be assured that Christ my Lord has redeemed me from hellish anxieties and torment by the unspeakable anguish, pains, and terrors which he suffered in his soul both on the cross and before" (4.044). The commentary on Christ's descent into hell does not mention hell as a future destination but refers to the hell we face on earth.

If heaven and hell figure as places in the Reformed confessions, they are hardly uniform destinations. Sometimes they figure most prominently as locations of blessedness and torment that await us after earthly life. At other times they refer to realities that we encounter in this life, when we walk by grace amid the struggles of life, struggles that we face with Christ as the pioneer of faith.

CALVIN, HELL, HEAVEN, AND THIS WORLD

In his *Institutes*, Calvin's interpretation of hell is brief, devoid of the detail common to much medieval theology. Most significantly, Calvin interprets hell as being "cut off from all fellowship with God" (3.25.12). The horror of hell, in his eyes, is not its supposed torments but separation from the life-giving relationship that is God's love. Moreover, the decisive torment occurs not to the wicked in hell but in Jesus Christ himself. The descent into hell is "an expression of the spiritual torment that Christ underwent for us. . . . He suffered the death that God in his wrath had inflicted upon the wicked!" (2.16.10). This descent, moreover, is testimony that Christ "did not shrink from taking our weaknesses upon himself" (2.16.12). In Calvin's theology Christ undergoes hell for our sake.

What, then, of heaven? Calvin's interpretation is likewise Christ-centered, signifying a heaven that God gives to us now. In the ascension, Christ's "body was raised up above all the heavens, so his power and energy were diffused and spread beyond all the bounds of heaven and earth" (2.16.14). As those who follow the crucified, risen, and ascended One, we do not simply await an inheritance in heaven but inherit the promise of heaven today: "Since he entered heaven in our flesh, as if in our name, it follows, as the apostle says, that in a sense we already 'sit with God in the heavenly places in him' so that we do not await heaven with a bare hope, but in our Head already possess it" (2.16.16). Calvin echoes this present understanding of heaven in his doctrine of the Lord's Supper, where in eating and drinking, we are gathered into heaven to receive the benefits of the kingdom: right here, right now. The Eucharist, for Calvin, is a heavenly meal, both because the ascended Christ is our host and because we are taken into his company through the food we receive and how we share it with others.[2] Heaven comes to earth and earth is invited into heaven whenever we eat and drink at Christ's table. For Calvin, Christ enters heaven "not to possess it by himself, but to gather you and all godly people with him" (4.17.27). He gives heaven to us.

For Calvin, heaven and hell are places that also describe relationships. They represent the enduring presence of relationship with the one God who gives life or the possibility that we can sever ourselves from that relationship. But unlike many expositions of heaven and hell of his time (including some of the subsequent Reformed confessions), Calvin describes heaven and hell chiefly as they relate to this life. Christians do not merely live in anticipation of heaven, exempting themselves from struggles for life and justice in this world. Rather, Christians seek conformity to Christ, by grace, in all facets of life. The Christian anticipates heaven not by longing for an afterlife but by living from and through the crucified, risen, and ascended Savior. He is the one who makes us inheritors of heaven: not simply at the end of days but now.

A REFORMED VIEW OF HEAVEN AND HELL

How might Reformed Christians in our day continue to talk about heaven and hell, especially when we don't share the cosmology of the biblical writers? First, we ought to acknowledge that no consistent portrait of heaven and hell emerges from the Bible as a whole. Instead of presenting a seamless account of the destinies of the righteous and the wicked at the end of earthly life, Scripture instead offers an abundance of images and hopes. Both Testaments are keenly aware of the power of death; both espouse hope in a God who is just and calls all to be accountable to divine justice; both point to God's faithfulness that is stronger than death. A biblical doctrine of hell is difficult to conjure up. Yes, images of fire and torment occur from time to time; but wherever they occur in Scripture, they do not emphasize the afterlife as much as they encourage hearers of the Word to turn toward life.

Related to these portrayals of hell is the person of Satan. Satan appears throughout Scripture as a minor character, though his role is extremely varied: as a heavenly accuser in God's service (Job 1:6–7), as Christ's tempter (Mark 1:13), and as a cosmic figure whom God defeats (Rev. 20:7–10). Scripture knows nothing of a devil who is lord of hell, a figure who rules the underworld, tormenting his subjects. We ought not to claim as much about Satan in our time; as a figure, he points to the unsettling and ever-present possibility that we can live in evil by turning away from God and choosing death.

The same variety in biblical portrayals can also be said about heaven: both Testaments bear witness to a hope that transcends death, which is not the final word in the cosmos. But when the Bible alerts us to heaven, it draws our simultaneous attention to the earth. We distort Jesus' proclamation of the kingdom of heaven if we render it a promise that chiefly concerns the afterlife. When Jesus called his hearers to repent, he also indicated that the kingdom arrived in his person. Heaven does not simply await us at the end of our days; it is the power of the new life given to us in light of Christ's resurrection. Yes, Scripture contains images of eternal blessedness for the righteous; yes, the Reformed confessions offer spatial and relational images of heaven. But the purpose of these images in Scripture and our tradition is not simply to pacify the hearer with the promise of an afterlife but to point to the power of resurrection that transcends death, a power given to us in this life. Unlike Alcorn's vision at the beginning of this chapter, we don't go to heaven as much as God brings heaven to us.

Second, heaven and hell do not point simply to destinations after our life ends; they encourage our immersion in this world. On this point, Calvin—who claimed that in Christ we already possess heaven—is especially helpful. Christian faith revolves around life: a life given by God, redeemed in Christ, animated by the Spirit. Christian faith throws us into the world, laboring for the life of the world. Heaven and hell remind us that the promise of life, of communion with God given in Christ, is eternal. We glimpse life in the face of our neighbors—when the hungry are fed, when those who mourn are consoled, and when the naked are clothed. Earthly life is certainly not the end of life; but without it, hope for eternal life is meaningless. The Christian doesn't wait around for heaven but welcomes it by grace, wherever life is embraced. Heaven indicates that communion abides: to turn toward communion is to live; to turn from it is to die. We experience hell, therefore, not simply as the absence of communion in the next life but in the agony and violence of a world that often destroys communion. But hell does not offer the final word.

On the far horizon of Christian hope is the promise that death and Hades are conquered (Rev. 20:14), revealed as nothing in light of God's gift of life.

Third, Scripture and the Reformed heritage tend to use relational rather than spatial imagery to describe heaven and hell. This is particularly significant when our modern cosmology differs markedly from biblical cosmologies. If we can no longer describe heaven as a place above us and hell as existing below us, we need only recall those parts of our tradition that describe hell and heaven in terms of our relationship with God and one another. Above us and all around us is the vastness of cosmic space, swirling galaxies, mysterious black holes, the dust of exploding stars, and the possibility of other universes. Below us is the earth's crust, its mantle, and a core of molten and hardened metal. Hell describes not some place beneath us but the possibility that we might choose to live according to the ways of death. Hell represents the lie that we can continue to live apart from God: our willful severing of relationship from the God who gives life. Heaven is the promise of eternal communion with God, encountered in this life and beyond death. In affirming both of them, we affirm the reality of life-giving relationships of grace as well as the life-negating destruction of relationships.

Christian faith, however, recognizes that hell does not have a power over and against God. We understand hell best when we situate it within the context of God's saving purposes. Hell and death, simply put, represent all that opposes God's grace; they undergo a second death and banishment in the coming of God (Rev. 20). Heaven, by contrast, *is* God's intent: the life-giving relationship that comes from God alone and that abides in eternity, enveloping us in God's triune love, conforming us to the love we were made for all along. Heaven means that our lives and the life of the world are fulfilled in love. For this reason, heaven—not hell—expresses the hope of Christian faith and the life of the Christian, not merely at the end of our days but throughout their earthly course.

QUESTIONS FOR DISCUSSION

1. Does shifting our understanding of heaven and hell away from reward and punishment affect how we understand salvation in Jesus Christ?
2. Is it important for Christians to confess Christ's descent into hell? Why or why not?
3. What are some implications for Christian life of describing heaven and hell as *places*?
4. What are some implications of describing heaven and hell as *relationships*?

8

What about the Millennium and Armageddon?

QUESTIONS OF VIOLENCE

Our coffeehouse comrades are at it again: "Religion is to blame for most of the wars in this world," sighed Mark. "Think of it. The current mess in Israel and Palestine, the ongoing strife in Northern Ireland, even the 'War on Terror' played out in Iraq, Afghanistan, and the United States: all of them have religious roots. And that isn't anything new. The history of Christianity and nearly every other religion are filled with the violence of one war after another. Think about the Crusades of the Middle Ages and the conquest of the Americas by Europeans at the dawn of the modern age. Both of them gained momentum from a group of 'righteous' Christians who wanted to extend their righteousness, their way of life, and their religion to other parts of the world. Christian beliefs often lead to violent acts."

"I fear that you're right," added Angela. "So much of this ugly history seems to be related to what Christians believe about the end of the world: that God will vindicate the righteous in a final battle against Satan and the powers of evil. When Christians are convinced that they're right, then nothing can stop them. They feel that they are acting on God's behalf."

"Now you're getting it. And that stuff is in the Bible, too," quipped Mark. "Have you read the book of Revelation lately? There's blood on nearly every page, and that's how the Bible ends. God triumphs in a holy war: Armageddon, where God's army crushes the forces of evil, followed by the millennium, where the righteous install a thousand-year reign. That's dangerous stuff. It's exactly that kind of thing—reading those Scriptures and seeing oneself and one's fellow believers within those stories as forces for 'good'—

that leads to things like the Crusades and the Conquistadores. Christians have their own version of jihad, and they find justification for it right in the Bible."

"Are you meaning to say that the Bible actually *justifies* violence?" asked Angela. "I'm not so sure. Couldn't it be that violence results from a misreading of the Bible? What about all of Jesus' sayings on behalf of peace? And his peaceful, nonviolent means of resistance against the religious and political authorities of his time? Isn't that what the Bible justifies?"

"No, I mean exactly what I said. The Bible does justify violence. By the end of it, that peaceful Jesus whom we see from time to time in the Gospels has now become a crusading militant, descending from the heavens, seeking his children, and destroying his innumerable enemies. The way the Bible ends makes a difference, and it has affected how the church understands itself in history. Christianity, like nearly every other religion, has an ugly legacy: wars and rumors of war, all carried out by people who felt they were right and that others were wrong and needed to be destroyed in the name of the truth. Christianity is to blame for much of the world's violence and that blame has a lot to do with those images of Armageddon and the millennium that occur at the end of the Bible."

"John Lennon might have had the right idea," Angela added. "You know, imagining no heaven, no hell, everyone living in peace."

As we fade out of the conversation, we can hear the refrains of "Imagine," echoed by one of the more famous skeptics—and voices for peace—of the twentieth century. What are we to make of it? To be sure, Mark and Angela are correct about a number of things: Religion lies at the root of countless wars throughout history. The current century is no different in this regard from many that have preceded it. Despite their teachings of peace—which are common to all of the great world religions—religions instill in their adherents a sense of "rightness" that often perceives "otherness" as a threat to truth. That perceived threat, moreover, has often led to violence against others: recall, in the U.S. context, the systemic attempts to destroy Native American cultures in the name of "truth and civilization" and the countless Native Americans slaughtered on battlefields in the name of Manifest Destiny. The Bible, moreover, supplies its own share of violence: from the first murder (Gen. 4) to the final defeat of evil (Revelation). Because the Bible is filled with violence, it is perhaps no surprise that Armageddon and the millennium appear near the end of its pages. Are these images, in effect, the ultimate justification for violence in the Christian tradition? How should we understand them in light of the violence elsewhere in Scripture? Do they make any sense among Christians who seek peace? What do Armageddon and the millennium *mean*? To those questions we now turn.

ARMAGEDDON?

If you've ever seen one of those infamous charts composed by dispensationalist Christians that offers a time line of the history of the universe, Armageddon typically plays a starring role. In most versions, Armageddon occurs near
the end of the time line as the decisive battle where the world's evil princes
assemble against God's army of righteousness. A plain in Israel, Armageddon
or Megiddo, represents the place where God will destroy the forces of evil
forever, in the mightiest battle of all. According to most of these charts, the
day of this battle will arrive sooner rather than later. Signs of the times that
are readily discernible today—the decline in public morality, the escalation of
violence on a worldwide scale, even natural catastrophes (such as Hurricane
Katrina and the South Asian tsunami)—indicate that this final battle will soon
envelop us.

Or so the time line goes. But is this account of Armageddon a fruitful
reading of its appearance in Scripture? Hardly. For all their assertions about
creating a "biblical" framework for understanding the "last things," dispensationalists combine conjecture and rather loose readings of Scripture in
describing a future battle. Let's look at Armageddon again.

First, the name itself appears only once in the Bible, in Revelation 16:16,
and it occurs not in the context of a decisive battle but amid a narration of
seven plagues unleashed upon the earth. The chief subject here is not a cosmic battle but a series of seven judgments that resemble the plagues visited
upon the Egyptians in Exodus. In Revelation, however, the plagues extend to
the whole earth rather than to a particular people in a specific place. These
plagues signal God's judgment against unfaithfulness. The term *Armageddon*—or more accurately, as the NRSV translates it, *Harmagedon* or "mountain of Megiddo"—occurs in relation to the sixth of these plagues: the drying
of the river Euphrates so that kings might assemble "for battle on the great
day of God the Almighty" (16:14). Revelation suffuses with military imagery,
but, interestingly, when it mentions Harmagedon, it does not name Harmagedon as the site of a conclusive battle. The city of Megiddo was the site of
some significant battles in ancient Israel's lore (Judg. 5:19; 2 Kgs. 23:29–30),
but it does not appear again in the book of Revelation.

In identifying Armageddon as the site of the culminating battle between
good and evil, dispensationalists make many assumptions, including the
assumptions that the place of the battle is significant and that Revelation is
preoccupied with battles. I've already called the first assumption into question.
Revelation does not identify any subsequent battle (most significantly, Rev.
19:11–21, which records the defeat of God's adversaries) with a particular
place. The second assumption, that battles themselves are significant, is also

problematic, as we shall soon see. Why? Because the book of Revelation actually subverts rather than glorifies violence, even in the name of righteousness. Focusing on Armageddon, in other words, has more in common with Hollywood summer blockbusters than a biblical understanding of the last things. The dispensationalists don't even get the transliteration of the term right.

THE MILLENNIUM?

In most dispensationalist time lines, besides Armageddon, another event appears prominently: the millennium, a thousand-year reign of the righteous that is the penultimate event before God vanquishes evil completely. Occurring after the defeat of the worldly princes but before the final defeat of Satan, the millennium is a foreshadowing of final blessedness. This thousand-year reign will be a time when the righteous gain ascendancy once again, signaling that the final end of all things is almost upon us. Or so the story goes. Yet when we examine Scripture carefully, questions relating to this millennial view emerge.

Look for the word "millennium" in Scripture, and you won't find it. The event typically referred to as *the* millennium appears in a brief narrative near the end of the book of Revelation (Rev. 20:4–6). To dispensationalists' credit, the event occurs, narratively at least, between a temporary sealing of the serpent "who is the Devil and Satan" (20:2) in a pit and Satan's final defeat (20:7–10). But the nature of this millennial kingdom is different from the glitzy portrayals often found in charts. John's vision emphasizes those who were beheaded "for their testimony to Jesus and for the word of God" as the ones who "came to life and reigned with Christ a thousand years" (20:4). Martyrs, not the righteous, rule in this kingdom. Revelation privileges the *victims* of violence rather than those who exert righteous violence. The millennial reign, in other words, does not foster the extension of violence in the name of what is good and true; instead, it remembers those who have died in the faith.

Dispensationalist readings of this narrative assume a literal thousand-year reign. This assumption is puzzling given the nature of apocalyptic literature, which emphasizes ecstatic visions and imaginative symbolism rather than precise events occurring at particular times. The book of Revelation is not a blueprint for the future but a symbolic narrative that demonstrates God's faithfulness to the church even amid horrific struggles and persecutions.

In literalizing the thousand-year reign of the righteous, dispensationalists ignore the more figurative and fluid understandings of time witnessed in Revelation and elsewhere in Scripture. Take 2 Peter, for instance: "But do not ignore this one fact, beloved, that with the Lord one day is like a thousand years, and a thousand years are like one day" (2 Pet. 3:8). Or Psalm 90:

> For a thousand years in your sight
>   are like yesterday when it is past,
> or like a watch in the night.
>
> You sweep them away; they are like a dream,
> like grass that is renewed in the morning;
> in the morning it flourishes and is renewed;
> in the evening it fades and withers.
>   vv. 4–5

The length, time, and means of the millennial reign are not the point. Rather, the point is to remember the victims of violence: that their voices, souls, and presence will not be extinguished, despite the intent of their murderers. Their voices, in the end, will be heard. In this regard, the thousand-year reign is the beginning of the end of violence, religious or otherwise. In the end, the "millenium" has less to do with the final victory of the righteous than it has to do with God's remembering the voices of those long ago silenced by the sword.

THE LAMB WHO WAS SLAIN

The more significant issue behind the questions about Harmagedon and the millennium, in my opinion, is whether the book of Revelation and Christian understandings of Christ's coming sanction and breed violence. We ought to take seriously the conclusion that troubled our coffeehouse compatriots at the beginning of this chapter. Mark noticed something troubling: the book of Revelation contains more than its share of violence—some of it committed by evil powers; some of it, seemingly, by the righteous. This book, perhaps more than any other in sacred Scripture, has served as warrant—consciously or unconsciously—for violence against "others." Is Revelation the Christian equivalent of jihad? How does it understand violence? Despite—and perhaps because of—the blood saturating its pages, I offer an alternative read of Revelation as a voice against violence and for achieving victory through decisively nonviolent means.

Revelation consistently remembers the victims of violence rather than sanctioning violence in the name of the right. Foremost in its remembrance is the central figure of the book, the Lamb who was slain, a clear reference to the crucified Christ. The Lamb, in John's vision, is the Lord of history. Jesus Christ, as we read at the outset of the book is "the faithful witness, the firstborn of the dead, and the ruler of the kings of the earth" (1:5). This Lamb is the one who unfurls the seven seals that begin the sequence of judgments against the unfaithful, but his means of judgment does not repeat the cycle of the world's violence. Rather, the Lamb suffers at the hands of that violence. Christ's blood repeatedly fills the pages of the book. The faithful honor Christ by remembering the violence inflicted against God's anointed One:

> "Worthy is the Lamb that was slaughtered
> to receive power and wealth and wisdom and might
> and honor and glory and blessing!"
>
> Rev. 5:12

> "You are worthy to take the scroll
> and to open its seals,
> for you were slaughtered and by your blood you ransomed for God
> saints from every tribe and language and people and nation;
> you have made them to be a kingdom and priests serving our God,
> and they will reign on earth."
>
> Rev. 5:9–10

We honor Christ not because of his violent victory over the forces of evil but because he has been slain by them. The first word in the victory of the forces of good is remembrance—of violence inflicted. This is a strange way of battling, indeed: that God triumphs not by means of the most lethal weapons but in a remembrance of a slain Lamb who overturns violence, rendering it empty in his resurrection from the grave.

This slain Lamb does not assemble like-minded righteous warriors to battle against threats posed by different "others" but summons saints from every people and tribe on earth. This Lamb gathers together every language and tongue that is known. Recall the vision of the new Jerusalem where "its lamp is the Lamb. The nations will walk by its light" (Rev. 21:23–24). Here is a place where others are welcomed. This polyglot gathering is present earlier in the narrative, "a multitude that no one could count, from every nation, from all tribes and peoples and languages, standing before the throne and before the Lamb, robed in white, with palm branches in their hands" (7:9). This gathering of a multitude again subverts violence, as we read that their robes have been made white by washing them in the blood of the Lamb (7:14). Here dipping one's robe in blood yields cleanness rather than bloodthirstiness. Here the very logic of violence stands questioned. The slaughter of this one innocent victim, the Lamb, does not result in cries of revenge against the perpetrators but in the stopping of blood's flow, symbolized in white. The author is doubtless referring to the forgiveness of sins: Christ's death, the ultimate sacrifice, results in the cleansing of the multitude's sins. But the narrative also suggests that the violence that feeds on itself must also end: Those cleansed by the blood of the Lamb are not led out into battle against the wicked but are led to worship, hungering and thirsting no more, guided to the water of life, with every tear wiped from their eyes (7:15–17). The Lamb does not continue the cycle of the world's violence but ceases it in rising from the grave. Over him, and over the whole of creation, violence can only reign temporarily.

VIOLENCE IN THE BOOK

I do not mean to claim that the book of Revelation is devoid of violence. More blood flows here than in any other book in the New Testament, and probably in all of Scripture. I merely mean to call into question the logic of violence that many visions of the "end times" continue to espouse. Most time lines of the end accept violence as a means by which God acts in history, perhaps most decisively and violently at the "end" of history. Violence and war certainly occur in the book of Revelation, but how do they occur?

The judgments against the earth, represented in the plague visions (Rev. 8:2–9:21 and 15:1–16:21), are striking not in the violence represented by the sword but in the destruction wrought by the natural elements of creation: hail, earthquake, fire, wormwood, locusts, and the darkening of sun and stars. The violence that occurs through military means is committed by four angels who are "released" (9:15), suggesting that these are evil angels who had been bound by God. To cite such plagues as warrant for a godly, militaristic triumph over the unrighteous is questionable, to say the least. Certainly death occurs as a result of these plagues—a third of humankind (9:18)—but the violence that occurs is strangely built into the cycles of creation and the overextension of evil.

War also occurs in the book of Revelation, such as in chapter 12, where Michael and his angels fight against the dragon in heaven (12:7). This war, however, occurs in heaven rather than on earth and does not enlist the faithful to battle against the unfaithful but instead reveals the nonviolence of God's just reign. The angels defeat the dragon not through more effective use of violence but by reversing violence's course:

> "They have conquered him by the blood of the Lamb
>   and by the word of their testimony,
>   for they did not cling to life even in the face of death."
>   Rev. 12:11

In this "war," victory is accomplished through the blood of a victim and faithful words.

The decisive "battle," however, appears later in the book, though it is strikingly absent of military detail (Rev. 19:11–21). Although preparations for battle occur, the battle itself never really does. Instead of justifying religious violence, the text displays in symbol the cosmic dimensions of Christ's death and resurrection, the slain Lamb who conquers sin and death. Armies of heaven appear, led by a rider on a white horse. His clothing is a robe dripping in blood, a reminder of his atoning sacrifice, and his name is the Word of God. This horseman wields a sword not in his hand but in his mouth, indicating that his Word is mightier than all the weapons the kings can muster, destroying those who have waged war against the Lamb. When confronted with the Word of truth, the kings' powers are empty, destined for the lake of fire and the sword of his mouth. Far from sanctioning holy war, this final "battle" points to the emptiness of the world's violence in light of Christ's death and resurrection. The decisive event is not some future holy war but the victory over sin and death already achieved in Jesus Christ.

THE POWERS

Like no other book in Scripture, Revelation illustrates that Christian hope concerns not individual souls, and not merely the life of the Christian community, but the life of the universe. John's apocalyptic vision is populated with beasts that bestow death and unleash chaos, a Lamb slain who grants life in fullness, and a history-changing struggle between them. Jesus' life, death, resurrection, and return shake earthly powers to their core. He struggles against the powers in heaven and on earth that destroy life and reveals himself as the Power of the universe made manifest in weakness on the cross. Whereas the powers sustain themselves by holding fast to themselves, seizing others, the power of Christ reveals itself in letting go: "'Those who try to make their life secure will lose it, but those who lose their life will keep it'" (Luke 17:33).

Jesus understood that his coming would shake heaven and earth. In Luke, when he addresses the coming Son of Man, he claims,

> "There will be signs in the sun, the moon, and the stars, and on the earth distress among the nations confused by the roaring of the sea and the waves. People will faint from fear and foreboding of what is coming upon this world, for the powers of the heaven will be shaken." (Luke 21:25–26)

Even when those around him fail to discern the struggle at hand—as religious leaders try him and Pilate sentences him—the struggle still occurs, recognized most clearly by surprising characters, such as the centurion who proclaims at Jesus' death, "'Truly this man was God's Son!'" (Mark 15:39). Here, the consummate outsider—the soldier of empire—makes an unqualified confession of Jesus as the Christ that we don't even hear from the lips of the disciples. Recognizing the power and recognizing who is the One with power apparently does not depend on whether one is an "insider" to the discipleship community.

The Letter to the Ephesians narrates these powers even more strikingly: "For our struggle is not against enemies of blood and flesh, but against the rulers, against the authorities, against the cosmic powers of this present darkness, against the spiritual forces of evil in the heavenly places" (Eph. 6:12). Against these powers, readers are to "take up the whole armor of God" (6:13). But what are these powers? Demons and beings populating the cosmos? Armies of the evil one? Yes and no. The New Testament often personifies the powers as beings that inhabit a lively, three-tiered cosmos. But we misunderstand their scope if we understand them only as celestial or infernal beings. What Ephesians describes are events, movements, and people that vie for our allegiance. Powers demand our loyalty and obeisance, luring us away from God. The power of evil and destruction work insidiously by claiming our ultimate allegiance under the guise of the "good," often appealing to our fears. Hence, the good of "national identity" led to the murder of millions seen as "threats" to that identity in Nazi Germany. Hence, the "good" of "national security" in the United States leads to the construction of a border wall and escalating prejudice against immigrants. We don't understand the nature of systemic evil or the powers simply by focusing on individuals. The destructive power of Nazi Germany cannot be reduced to Adolf Hitler; the scourge of racism in the United States is not synonymous with the current Grand Wizard of the Ku Klux Klan. Powers transcend people, and that is what makes them potentially destructive. They change a group of angry people into a violent mob. What makes the power of racism so destructive is not that it is located only within an aberrant group of racists; what makes it destructive is how it takes root throughout society and summons our allegiance in disguised forms (such as protecting the "American way of life"), affecting literally *everything* in society. Imprisoning the current Grand Wizard will not counter racism in American society, only a struggle against its power in every form will.

Ephesians is aware of the scope of every power. But this letter also assures us that the struggle against the powers will lead to victory because Christ unmasks them, exposing their falsehood. No matter what vies for our allegiance, those claims of allegiance are ultimately empty: "God put this power to work in Christ when he raised him from the dead and seated him at his right hand in the heavenly places, far above all rule and authority and power and dominion, and above every name that is named, not only in this age, but in the age to come" (1:20–21). The struggle against the powers doesn't simply await the world at the end of the age; it presents itself every moment of every day. If Christian hope envisions Harmagedon, it also recognizes the significance of every effort on behalf of humanity, on behalf of the life of the planet itself in the face of the power of death and sin. We don't simply await victory when Christ returns; we participate in victory right now as we are girded with the armor of God and the power of Christ made manifest in weakness.

The powers, whether now or in the age to come, are subject to Christ (1 Pet. 3:22). Against them we have nothing to fear. "The strife is o'er, the battle done, the victory of life is won," chimes the old Easter hymn. What we sing on Easter we also proclaim in the face of the powers. They are real. They destroy and kill. But God remembers their victims even when we do not, carrying the victims to participate in God's very life. Christian hope in triumph over the powers does not mean that tragedy disappears from the face of the earth; it simply means that tragedy does not have the final word. The grandest hope of all is that nothing can separate us from the love of God in Christ, no power indeed:

> For I am convinced that neither death, nor life, nor angels, nor rulers, nor things present, nor things to come, nor powers, nor height, nor depth, nor anything else in all creation, will be able to separate us from the love of God in Christ Jesus our Lord. (Rom. 8:38–39)

Harmagedon and the millennium are not blueprints for events in the far-off or not-so-distant future. They are vivid, symbolic depictions of what Christians encounter every day of their lives: a struggle against death, epitomized in powers of heaven and earth. But in Christ, we are assured that no power holds sway against the cross and resurrection; in the face of Christ's power, made manifest in weakness, all other powers are empty.

QUESTIONS FOR DISCUSSION

1. Is violence ever justified in Christian life? Why or why not?
2. The book of Revelation contains battle imagery (12:7–17; 16:8–21; 19:11–21). What is the relationship of these images to Christ, the Prince of Peace?
3. The conclusion to this chapter focuses on "the powers." How in your life do you experience conflict or confrontation with what Scripture calls the powers?

9

What about the Antichrist?

HISTORICAL MISUNDERSTANDINGS

"Ronald Reagan was the antichrist," exclaimed Steve during the church coffee hour. A small group had gathered around him. Steve was known in the church for making bold—and controversial—proclamations. The group gathered around him had just finished a Bible study of the book of Revelation. Many in the group had become somewhat agitated, convinced that the "end times" were upon them, seeking to discern "signs of the times" in contemporary events and political figures. Steve continued his thoughts, "The book of Revelation tells us that the mark of the beast is the number 666. Do you know what Reagan's full name was? Ronald Wilson Reagan. Each name has six letters. If you convert the letters to numbers, you get the number 666. Reagan claimed to be religious, but he really was not. He presided over a dramatic growth of the U.S. military, as if preparing for a final showdown. All of that convinces me that he was the antichrist."

"Aw, come on, Steve!" protested Amir. "It wasn't Reagan at all. You're looking in the wrong direction. The antichrist must be avowedly anti-Christian. And what is the most anti-Christian force in the world right now? Communism. The antichrist will come under the guise of helping people and will propose an entire system that substitutes itself for faith in God. He will demand total allegiance, and his subjects will blindly follow him. I'm not comfortable singling out one communist person as the antichrist, but I'm pretty sure he will espouse the communist system. Maybe it was Chairman Mao; maybe it was Stalin; maybe it's Castro or Kim Jong-il. All are communists; all encouraged the development of a cult of personality; all blaspheme Christianity; and all are responsible in some way for massive increases in military might, as if preparing for Armageddon. Each of them seems a more likely candidate for the antichrist than Reagan."

"Wait a minute, friends," chimed in Maria. "You're missing something important. You're both focusing on past threats to Christianity. Communism has had its day; Reagan is dead. What about the present threats? It's clear to me that the number one threat to our faith is Islam. The antichrist will come as one of those ayatollahs, a man of supposedly sincere faith who is bent on destruction: jihad and all that stuff. Where do you think the terrorists get their motivation? From these religious extremists who pretend they come in peace but come only to destroy. And they're out to destroy us, our faith, and our way of life. The antichrist will surely be Muslim."

"I think the antichrist will come from a Christian place: looking and acting like a Christian but clandestinely undermining everything about Christian faith," claimed Paul. "I think the most likely place he will arise is Eastern Europe. The book of Daniel mentions something about trouble arising in the East. Maybe even the antichrist will be gay: you know, there are lots of gays who pretend they are Christian."

"Oh, come on now," complained Sarah, "I don't believe any of you at all. The antichrist has to be the pope: the one who proclaims himself God's instrument; the one who claims to be the foremost Christian of all. This is substituting oneself for Christ, demanding worship as if one were Christ. This is what Scripture warns against. We don't need to look outside the church to find the antichrist. We find him in the church."

As we leave this argument, our participants continue in the same vein: each claiming to have special insight—whether by reading Scripture or by discerning the signs of the times—to make a claim about the antichrist. Perhaps you've heard something along these lines before. An Internet search of "antichrist" will yield multiple Web sites that include *all* of these proposals and conjectures. But before we proceed any further, it is important to recognize from the outset how much *fear* motivates these participants to make a pronouncement about the antichrist. Each of the conversation partners has determined a "threat" to Christian faith by a particular person or by a certain group of persons. When they do so, they perpetuate a long history of Christian xenophobia (fear of others). The history of the church, sadly, is peppered with hundreds of examples of such Christian prejudice: Women who questioned church custom were deemed "witches" and burned at the stake; Native Americans who engaged in rich religious practices before the arrival of Europeans were considered "savages" who had to be converted; gays were deemed "sodomites" and "perverts" who flaunted faith in their bodies; Africans were deemed unable to understand the gospel and only suited for slavery and lynching. Each of the participants in this coffee-hour conversation perpetuates some of that history, though in perhaps more subtle ways. The most likely candidate for the antichrist appears as that person or group that one fears the most: communists, gays, Muslims, Catholics.

The first thing to say about this disturbing tendency toward fearmongering is that it has to stop, as it is antithetical to the kingdom that Jesus proclaimed. Jesus' incarnation in first-century Palestine and his final return are not for a select group bent on excluding others. He welcomes all in radical gestures of hospitality as the One who dines with tax collectors and sinners, inviting us to overcome our fears of others, inviting others to share food and drink.

Our conversation participants also err in their discussion by focusing on religious or political figures as "the" antichrist who summons our allegiance. This, however, is something that the New Testament does *not* do. The best place to begin a discussion of the antichrist and its significance for Christian hope is with the New Testament. What do we find there? Fairly little, but most of it is sufficient to question the entire coffee-hour conversation we have just heard.

WHO IS THE ANTICHRIST? SCRIPTURAL MUSINGS

References to the term *antichrist* surface rather infrequently in the New Testament: in three distinct places in two short letters attributed to John (1 John 2:18–23; 4:1–3; 2 John 7). Nowhere else does *antichrist* appear in Scripture: not in Revelation, not in the Gospels, not in Paul's letters. There is little evidence, moreover, of the term appearing in Christian literature prior to these letters. Perhaps the author of the letters invented the term; perhaps he drew on earlier usage within the churches he addressed. Suffice it to say that his uses of the term are unique in Scripture. Let's look at each of the three passages.

Antichrist first appears in a warning about the "last hour," which the author claims is upon the readers. The author, moreover, uses the term in the plural, suggesting that *antichrist* cannot be reduced to a particular figure: "As you have heard that antichrist is coming, so now many antichrists have come" (1 John 2:18). The author's description, moreover, indicates not aliens to the community but ones who have come, at least originally, from the community itself and claim allegiance to it: "They went out from us, but they did not belong to us; for if they had belonged to us, they would have remained with us. But by going out they made it plain that none of them belongs to us" (2:19). One way to challenge our coffee-hour conversationalists, therefore, is to say that any talk about "the" antichrist who constitutes an outside threat is unbiblical! The first appearance of the term in Scripture suggests *several* antichrists who claim to belong not to another system or religion but to the church itself.

What are the marks of these antichrists? Instead of the conjectures offered by our coffee-hour conversationalists, John singles out false teaching. He names, moreover, two *specific* false teachings: denial of Jesus as the Christ and denial of the Father and the Son (1 John 2:22). Denying these central teachings of Christian faith threatens the fabric of the church. Beyond this description of false teaching, however, we do not have much detail. But his warning drives us back to the incarnation: to Jesus the anointed One of God, Savior of the world who comes in the flesh.

John encourages the community to discern the presence of antichrists by testing their spirits, assessing their teaching according to whether they stress the coming of Jesus in the flesh:

> Beloved, do not believe every spirit, but test the spirits to see whether they are from God; for many false prophets have gone out into the world. By this you know the Spirit of God: every spirit that confesses that Jesus Christ has come in the flesh is from God, and every spirit that does not confess Jesus is not from God. And this is the spirit of the antichrist, of which you have heard that it is coming. (1 John 4:1–3)

The greatest danger to the church's teaching, in this view, is denying that Christ came in the flesh, in *our* flesh. Perhaps the antichrists in John's day were Gnostics; perhaps they were others who held that it demeaned God to become incarnate in a human being. Perhaps they wanted to preserve God's majesty by denying that Jesus Christ was with the Father. But John indicates that the denial of the flesh and the denial of Jesus with the Father is a betrayal of faith: "No one who denies the Son has the Father; everyone who confesses the Son has the Father also" (1 John 2:23). For John, the fleshiness of the gospel matters: God seeks us, restlessly, relentlessly, in the flesh. In the end, John's discussion of the antichrist is another affirmation of the body. Perhaps the commandment we can extract from it is "Do not despise the body." Why? Because the body is what Christ assumed, what Christ became, for our sake. Antichrists deny the body—perhaps out of holiness, perhaps out of fear. Those who know Christ know that he has come in the flesh, to redeem, bless, and sustain us as bodies, now and eternally. To deny that Jesus came in the flesh is to deny the Son and the Father: "Many deceivers have gone out into the world, those who do not confess that Jesus Christ has come in the flesh; any such person is the deceiver and the antichrist!" (2 John 7). This is a far cry from our coffee-hour conversation!

If these are the only passages that mention antichrists in all of Scripture, how did that figure adopt such a different persona in the history of the church? Speculation about the antichrist, after all, is not unique to the present day. What happened is that many in the church combined these explicit references to antichrists with other biblical passages that speak of deceivers. Second Thessalonians, for example, speaks apocalyptically of a lawless one who "exalts himself above every so-called god or object of worship . . . declaring himself to be God" (2:3–4). Revelation, as we have already heard, speaks of a beast and a dragon, references most likely to Rome (Rev. 12–13). The Gospel of Mark, in an apocalyptic passage, refers to a "desolating sacrilege," a reference to the pagan destruction of the Temple in Jerusalem (Mark 13:14). And Daniel, full of apocalyptic symbolism of horns and beasts, describes the kind of cosmic struggle that we discovered in the previous chapter. The church slowly identified antichrist with these and other figures, and the term took on political and religious hues. In times of persecution and struggle, many in the church found refuge by identifying political powers and other religious movements as "antichrists." But in doing so, they also departed from the core biblical teaching about antichrists: denial that Jesus came in the flesh. The church's history of labeling persons and events as antichrists, accordingly, reveals more about our fears than our hopes.

REFORMED HERITAGE: HISTORICAL SUSPICION AND CONTEMPORARY SILENCE

Teachings about antichrists have never occupied a great deal of Reformed attention. But as a movement that experienced its own persecution (as well as meting it out against others), our Reformed forbears were sometimes quick to find the antichrist in their midst. The only Reformed confession to mention the antichrist does so in one paragraph: the Second Helvetic Confession (5.074). On the positive side, this reference occurs within a discussion of Christ's death, resurrection, and ascension. Following the lead I have already outlined, the confession situates discussion of antichrist within a larger discussion of the *body* of Christ. But it also leaves that outline behind as it speculates about the antichrist's identity: "From heaven the same Christ will return in judgment, when wickedness will then be at its greatest in the world and when the Antichrist, having corrupted true religion, will fill up all things with superstition and impiety and will cruelly lay waste the church with bloodshed and flames." The biblical reference here is Daniel 11, a passage that does not mention antichrists. Moreover, even though the confession does not specify names for antichrist, it is reasonable to suspect that the instigator of "superstition," who corrupts "true religion," was the Roman Catholic Church.

The Reformers commonly hurled accusations against the Catholic Church; Catholics hurled their own accusations in return. Both were antichrists to each other. Second Helvetic rehashes these polemics once again. What happens in the Second Helvetic Confession happens again and again throughout the history of the church: some attention is given to biblical tradition but also to a combination of disparate apocalyptic figures, locating the danger outside one's own faith community. Daniel's beast becomes John's antichrist, who then becomes identified with a contemporary figure or movement. We then find antichrist in someone else, forgetting that antichrist concerns false teachings over Jesus' flesh rather than political or ecclesial struggles.

Though Calvin does not devote much attention to antichrist in the *Institutes*, he echoes this tendency to label others. For him, the pope is antichrist. Calvin summons a litany of evidence for his assertions that has become hackneyed in our day: The pope is the antichrist because "his seat is placed in the Temple of God" (4.2.12). The pope "has shamelessly transferred to himself what belonged to God alone and especially to Christ," and "we should have no doubt that he is the leader and standard-bearer of that impious and hateful Kingdom" (4.7.25). Calvin proposes that the beginnings of the bishopric in Rome were faithful and true, but that it became the kingdom of the antichrist when the Roman bishop declared himself to be universal bishop, which Calvin claims happened in the reign of Pope Boniface III at the beginning of the seventh century. For this supposed demise, Calvin has harsh words: "By making their pontiff universal they declare him to be Antichrist" (4.7.21). In these writings, Calvin displays venom common to the Age of Reform. In the interest of demonstrating the truth of Reformed understandings of the church and his concern with present and past abuses in the Roman Catholic Church, he feels compelled to name the "depravity" of the papacy. Though he claims that a faithful remnant remains in the Roman Catholic Church throughout the ages, his sixteenth-century comments about the papacy have plagued Reformed-Catholic relations ever since. There is hardly a Reformed Christian on the planet who has not at one time heard the epithet of antichrist uttered against the pope. Not only are Calvin's reflections on antichrist infected with anti-Catholic bias, but he is also guilty of a rather free combination of disparate biblical themes. For example, he explicitly equates antichrist with the "lawless one" of 2 Thessalonians (4.9.4). In light of this ugly history, we ought to read Calvin's words on antichrist with extreme suspicion.

The most important theme to salvage from Calvin's otherwise disturbing interpretation of antichrist is his strong affirmation of the limited scope of his reign. Whatever antichrist represents—falsehood, pride, evil—the kingdom of

God brings to naught. When we pray according to the Lord's Prayer, "Thy kingdom come," we reveal the emptiness of antichrist's kingdom. In this prayer, says Calvin, God "overthrows the wicked conspiracies of enemies, unravels their stratagems and deceits, opposes their malice, represses their obstinacy, until at last he slays Antichrist with the Spirit of his mouth, and destroys all ungodliness by the brightness of his coming" (3.20.42). Praying as Jesus taught us, we do not fear antichrist but know that his reign will end.

GUIDELINES FOR CONTEMPORARY FAITH

In the centuries since Calvin's writing of the *Institutes*, Reformed teaching on antichrist has ebbed and flowed. At present, despite the emergence of the Left Behind books, Reformed Christianity—at least in the West—has tended toward silence on the subject. Very few introductory theological texts or dictionaries written from a Reformed perspective even mention antichrist. As a result, a topic that Scripture addresses gets left to fundamentalist, dispensationalist, and millenarian groups. This silence has left many Reformed Christians in a state of confusion, wondering whether the entire concept of antichrist is an outmoded relic of an earlier stage of Christianity or whether the more conservative branches of Christianity are correct in holding onto this idea. When silence appears, however, words begin to fill in gaps. Is antichrist a figure that sustains or minimizes Christian hope? I believe the figure is worth preserving, so long as it is held lightly and without the tendency toward identifying specific figures as antichrist that has so often plagued the church's history. In clarifying what antichrist is, however, it may be most helpful to identify what it is *not*.

First, antichrist is not a religious-imperial figure—present or past—who summons all allegiance to himself. Nothing of the kind is found in the three instances in Scripture where antichrist is mentioned. In the history of the church, antichrist developed into such a concept, which was the result of a creative combination of biblical texts and experiences of persecution—and perhaps paranoia—in various Christian communities. We ought to reject outright any claim that antichrist is a specific person—the pope, a political leader, or an imam.

Second, antichrist should not be confused with other apocalyptic figures that appear in Scripture. Antichrist is *not* the devil, *not* the beast of Revelation, and *not* one of the apocalyptic figures that populate the book of Daniel. The oddity of many fundamentalist Christians is that their claim for a "biblical" understanding of antichrist pays very little attention to the specific context and identity of antichrist in John's letters. There we find no equation between antichrist and other biblical figures.

What, then, is antichrist? Primarily it is a teaching that emerges from those who claim to be speaking for the church, a teaching that denies the incarnation. In contrast to antichrist, Christians proclaim *that Jesus Christ came in the flesh and that to know him is to know the God who sent him.* This basic claim has sustained Christian faith for centuries. Denial of it disparages the body and distorts Christian faith. John is concerned not with named people who threaten faith but with teachings that leads us away from the One who comes in the flesh. And if we follow those false teachings, we are led away from the ground of our redemption and salvation. When Gregory of Nazianzus wrote in the fourth century, "For that which he has not assumed he has not healed,"[1] he meant that if Jesus Christ did *not* come in the flesh, taking our flesh fully and completely as his own, then we are *not* saved. The good news of Christian faith, however, is that Jesus Christ did come in the flesh and that he will come again. Because of his incarnation, crucifixion, resurrection, and return, we are redeemed. That is surely good news for bodies broken in our age, enough to sustain hope now and in the years to come, whatever may come.

QUESTIONS FOR DISCUSSION

1. Why is it important for the church to proclaim that Jesus comes in the flesh?
2. Where have you heard the term *antichrist*, and how does what you've heard differ from the interpretation offered in this chapter?
3. Why have Christians throughout the ages often labeled their enemies as antichrists? How are we tempted to make these labels today?

PART IV

Living Hope

Christian hope concerns the present as much as it does the future. Christians anticipate not the destruction of the world as we know it but its renewal by grace. But if Christian hope for the future entails hope for the present, what does that mean in practice? How are Christians to live as hopeful people today in light of what we believe about tomorrow? To these questions we now turn, with a special focus on the two sacraments in the Reformed tradition: baptism and the Lord's Supper. God sustains our hope in both practices as they transform our living in the world, from how we share food to how we grow in grace. These practices are not confined to the sanctuary but spill into the world, renewing hope and renewing lives.

10

Baptism

When I was in elementary school, some friends and I sometimes would play a risky game at a local swimming pool. Armed with high-tech digital watches, we would compete to see who could hold his breath underwater the longest. One afternoon when we were playing this game, I was eager to prove my mettle. I inhaled deeply, then submerged myself in the deep end of the pool, flapping my arms upward to keep my body below water. I felt the first urge to surface and ignored it; then I ignored the second urge; finally, when I could stand it no longer I rushed to the surface, gasping for air, breathing so deeply that I felt that I could swallow the sky. I have no idea who won that particular game, but I do remember how relieved I was to be gulping fresh air again. A bit dazed from the performance, I felt like I had gained a new lease on life. After that, I didn't play the game ever again.

Something happens in baptism akin to what I experienced in the deep end of the pool many summers ago, but on a far grander scale. But just what do we believe about baptism? For many of us, the simplest definition of baptism is that it is a rite of church membership, something the church does to show our incorporation into the body of Christ. Denominations practice baptism differently, with some, such as Presbyterians, Lutherans, and Roman Catholics, advocating infant baptism as a sign of God's grace in incorporating us as members of Christ's body. Others, such as Mennonites and the Church of Christ, practice adult believer's baptism as a testimony of faith for which we must be accountable. Baptism signals that we belong to Christ, but it also shows that we participate in events that sustain Christian hope: namely, the life, death, and resurrection of Jesus Christ. In baptism, we die and are raised to new life, not simply in the singular baptismal event but again and again as we live in light of our baptism. Although what I experienced in the deep end of the pool many summers ago felt like a kind of baptism, when we are truly baptized, we die with Christ in submersion and are released with him in resurrection as we surface, gasping and struggling for new life, knowing that we have a new lease on life by grace. Baptism is more than a membership card in the church. It represents how we as a people participate in the eschatological events of Christ's death and resurrection, events that shake the course of heaven and earth.

THE BAPTISM OF JESUS

In order to answer the question "What is baptism?" we must first look at Jesus' baptism. Something happens to Jesus in baptism, which in turn happens to *us*. Each of the Gospels record John the Baptist's baptism of Jesus, each with particular emphases. John, for example, is unique in recording not the *event* of Jesus' baptism but John the Baptist's remembrance of that event. But all of the Gospels capture something of Jesus' submission to baptism and the cosmic nature of that event. Nowhere in the Gospels does Jesus baptize someone else; in each Gospel, he submits to baptism. We see this position of willing submission, of handing oneself over to another, repeatedly in the life of Jesus, culminating in his death on a cross. Jesus submits to baptism for the life of the world.

Jesus' baptism is also a *cosmic* event:

> And when Jesus had been baptized, just as he came up from the water, suddenly the heavens were opened to him and he saw the Spirit of God descending like a dove and alighting on him. And a voice from heaven said, "This is my Son, the Beloved, with whom I am well pleased." (Matt. 3:16–17)

In Jesus' baptism, earth opens to heaven, and heaven, to earth. All creation and the glory of God—human beings, dove, water, sky, and a heavenly voice—attest to Jesus' baptism. This baptism is not simply something that happens to Jesus but to waters that quench the earth, humans who populate the earth, doves that sing to the earth, and the One who sustains and renews the earth. The church also witnesses in this narrative one of the few occasions in all Scripture that depicts the triune life (Spirit as dove, Son as Jesus, Father as voice). Jesus' baptism is thus a Trinitarian event as well as an event of creation. Something about it gives new life to the world.

After his baptism, Jesus occasionally refers to it. But when he does, he understands it not simply as an event contained in the past. Rather, he continually undergoes baptism, and the disciples must experience it as well. In the Gospel of Mark, after Jesus foretells his death and resurrection for the third time, James and John come to him requesting places of honor in glory. His response to them reframes their request: "You do not know what you are asking. Are you able to drink the cup that I drink, or be baptized with the baptism that I am baptized with?" (Mark 10:37–38). Jesus' baptism is also *their* baptism. His lot is also their lot: baptism by water *and* participation in his death and resurrection. Jesus' baptism is also a *present* event.

Jesus also understands his baptism as a sign of judgment, connected to the coming of God's reign. In Luke, Jesus regards his baptism as something that has not yet occurred: " 'I came to bring fire to the earth, and how I wish it were already kindled! I have a baptism with which to be baptized, and what stress I am under until it is completed!' " (Luke 12:49–50). Here Jesus anticipates his death, suggesting that his baptism lies in the future as a sign of divine judgment that purifies the earth with fire. In the Gospels, Jesus' baptism encompasses past, present, and future. Jesus' baptism isn't something that happens to him once and then gets transferred to us; his baptism summons us as participants in the new reign he is inaugurating. What happens to Jesus is commanded of the disciples and offered to the world. Something happens in that baptism, but in it we also hope for something to happen, and that hope is for the new life of the world.

CLEANSING SIN

At its most basic level, baptism is a bath. Baptism takes a universal human practice, bathing, and endows it with deep religious symbolism. Water, perhaps the greatest necessity for life, becomes, in Augustine's words, God's "visible Word" to us as it cleanses us from sin and releases us for new life. The church generally interprets Jesus' baptism as baptism for us. He who was without sin underwent baptism for us as a token of his solidarity with us: becoming sin for our sake, undergoing baptism for our sake, bathed in the river for our sake. For Calvin, this washing is significant: "For baptism attests to us that we have been cleansed and washed" (*Institutes* 4.14.22). By these words Calvin does not mean that baptism erases sin from our lives, but rather that sin no longer reigns as the fundamental reality of life. We live, he claims, not by sin, but in and through Jesus Christ. We should have no illusion that sin does not continue in the lives of the baptized; sin remains and will remain until we pray in glorious communion with the One who underwent baptism for our sake. But we commence this struggle with sin confident that baptism abides. In this sense, baptism does not happen once in our lives, even if we are bathed in those waters, literally at least, one time. In Calvin's words, "We are not to think that baptism was conferred upon us only for a past time, so that for newly committed sins into which we fall after baptism we must seek new remedies of expiation. . . . We must realize that at whatever time we are baptized, we are once for all washed and purged for our whole life" (*Institutes* 4.15.3). Our baptism, in other words, accompanies us for the entire journey of life. The new thing that is present in baptism, forgiveness and cleansing of sin, is also testament to the old thing that God has always been up to in the world: inviting creation into covenant, offering new life every step of the way.

DYING AND RISING WITH CHRIST

The Gospels suggest that Jesus' baptism is also our baptism into his death and resurrection. That suggestion becomes explicit in Paul's letters. Romans contains one of the foremost examples: "Do you not know that all of us who have been baptized into Christ Jesus were baptized into his death? Therefore we have been buried with him by baptism into death, so that, just as Christ was raised from the dead by the glory of the Father, so we too might walk in newness of life" (Rom. 6:3–4; see also Col. 2:12). In baptism, we are submerged in the waters in death and then rise, gasping for new life, given new life by grace. For this transformation, nothing less than burial imagery will do: to be baptized is to die only to live again.

The Larger Catechism of the Westminster Confession offers another image of the connections between baptism, death, and resurrection: Baptism is a sacrament of remission of sins "and regeneration by his Spirit; of adoption, and resurrection unto everlasting life" (7.275). The Reformers are not often mistaken for mystics, Christians who attest to the believer's ecstatic union with God through Jesus Christ, but on the subject of baptism, they often speak in mystical ways. Calvin and others in the Reformed tradition write of believers intermingling in the person of Jesus Christ through baptism. The Scots Confession, for example, states, "By baptism we are engrafted into Christ Jesus, to be made partakers of his righteousness" (3.21), while Calvin claims that in baptism "we are not only engrafted into the death and life of Christ, but so united to Christ that we become sharers in all his blessings" (*Institutes* 4.15.6). Baptism does not simply happen to us; we become—in some sense— the happening itself. The life that we live, the death that we die, is Christ's, and ours through Christ. In baptism, moreover, the expression, "mine and mine alone," is no longer valid: "As many of you as were baptized into Christ have clothed yourself with Christ" (Gal. 3:27). The lives that we live are not our own; in baptism, they belong to others and to God through Jesus Christ.

The hope of Christian life—that we may be united with God in blessedness and to others in communion—has in fact already happened in baptism.

BAPTISM AS THE UNITING OF EAST AND WEST

We live in an age where the dividing lines between groups of people seem starker than ever. Despite the much-heralded era of globalization, which claims to unite persons across ethnic, cultural, and religious lines, the twenty-first century has witnessed more than its share of cultural division. From the massacre in Darfur to the ongoing struggle between Israelis and Palestinians; from the border fence in Texas to the threat of border war in Kosovo; from anti-immigration politics in North America and Europe to Hindu nationalism in India, the twenty-first century is marked by cultural division more than it is by intercultural understanding. Pick a continent, and one will find abundant examples of racism, internecine warfare, cultural prejudice, and religious persecution. The world is a far cry from the vision of hope that appears at the Bible's conclusion: a renewed city, a renewed earth, where the nations walk by the light of the glory of God. Christian hope, as it gathers steam from that vision, longs for the uniting of diverse peoples and practices baptism as a sign of that longing.

The risen Christ's last words to his disciples in the Gospel of Matthew convey this anticipation of a new age: " 'Go therefore and make disciples of *all nations*, baptizing them in the name of the Father and of the Son and of the Holy Spirit, and teaching them to obey everything that I have commanded you. And remember, I am with you always, to the end of the age' " (Matt. 28:19–20, emphasis added). Baptism is not a rite restricted to a particular people or culture; it expresses hope for the world, that all might be one in Christ.

This theme of one body pervades Paul's thoughts on the church and baptism: "For in the one Spirit we were all baptized into one body—Jews or Greeks, slaves or free—and we were all made to drink of one Spirit" (1 Cor. 12:13). The familiar hymn "In Christ There Is No East or West" also conveys this hope: that in baptism the divisions that have led to misunderstanding and even violence are overcome "in one great fellowship of love throughout the whole wide earth." In Christ, in baptism, all are children of God, united by his grace. Talk of oneness and unity, however, can easily become a mask for the imposition of one culture over another. Does the coming together of cultures in Christ—this meeting of East and West—mean the erasing of cultural differences? Is that what Christian hope envisions, a global monoculture heading toward the new Jerusalem?

If we look at the record of the early church's baptisms in Acts, the answer to that question is an emphatic "No." The most difficult issue the early church faced was whether Gentile converts to the Way should also follow Jewish law. This issue nearly led to schism, with Paul arguing against the necessity for Gentile Christians to follow Jewish law and other early leaders arguing for it. In part, the issue was over culture as well as religion. Should the culture of the first generation of Christians become the norm for all other disciples, no matter where they came from? The arguments were heated, and the confrontations, frequent: like the present-day church, the early church was hardly a model of uniform opinion! But the Council of Jerusalem reached a significant decision that has repercussions down to the present day: Gentile converts did not need to become adherents of Jewish law, so long as they refrained from idolatry, fornication, strangled animals, and blood (Acts 15:20). The decision, in effect, welcomed *all* cultures into the fold.

We see this welcome extended throughout the book of Acts, whenever baptisms appear. One of the first to be baptized in that book is an Ethiopian eunuch—no doubt a cultural stranger to the early Jewish Christians—who requests to be baptized by Philip (Acts 8:26–40). After this brief encounter, we hear nothing more from the eunuch, other than that he "went on his way rejoicing" (v. 39), presumably returning home (v. 28). Extracanonical legend attributes the founding of the Ethiopian Orthodox Church, one of the most ancient of Christian churches with its own unique practices, to this eunuch. Baptism conveys the identity of belonging to Christ. It cleanses us from sin and communicates our participation in Christ's death and resurrection, but it does not conform us to a particular culture.

Shortly after this baptismal scene, Peter, who initially argues for the circumcision of Gentiles and their adherence to the Law, experiences a vision that changes his mind and leads to the baptism of Gentiles (Acts 10:1–48). Praying on a roof, he falls into a trance and sees a table teeming with all kinds of unclean animals. He hears a voice commanding him to kill and eat, claiming, "'What God has made clean, you must not call profane'" (v. 15). Confounded by the vision, he eventually understands it to refer to the inclusion of Gentiles: "'Can anyone withhold the water for baptizing these people who have received the Holy Spirit just as we have?' So he ordered them to be baptized in the name of Jesus Christ" (vv. 47–48). If in Christ there is no East or West, this does not mean that East and West disappear. It means that the world's unique cultures are held together in Christ, not as antagonistic excuses for violence but as different experiences of the One Spirit. Baptism unites these cultures, offering hope for a world torn by intercultural violence.

IMPROVEMENT IN BAPTISM

The mending of a world wracked by violence has not yet occurred. Though we may be united to Christ's death and resurrection in baptism and may offer the world an alternative to violence in the practice of baptism, intercultural hatreds continue to run their destructive course. Baptism also announces a paradox of Christian life: it signifies the end of sin as the ruling principle of life but also sin's continuing remainder, which infects the lives of individuals, communities, churches, and the world as a whole. If baptism marks the end of sin as the guiding reality of life, it also marks the beginning of a lifelong struggle against sin, a struggle only undertaken by God's grace. The hope of baptism is not that it is an elixir or magical rite that erases sin from life. Rather, its hope causes us to glimpse sin for what it is: real, pervasive, enduring, but destined for nothing by grace. If sin continues its tenacious hold throughout our lives, its hold is temporary. Baptism is thus not a one-time event but the beginning of the new life of discipleship. In church, whenever baptisms are performed, believers make promises to those baptized and are called to remember their own baptisms. Baptisms don't end when the waters dry on our foreheads; that is, in a sense, when they begin.

The Westminster Confession echoes this progressive understanding of baptism when it states, "The efficacy of baptism is not tied to that moment of time wherein it is administered" (6.159). The entirety of the Christian life, read through the lens of baptism, is a lifelong dying and rising with Christ: "Baptism with water represents not only cleansing from sin, but a dying with Christ and a joyful rising with him to new life. It commits all Christians to die each day to sin and to live for righteousness" (Confession of 1967, 9.51). Christians remember their baptisms daily, as we are sent out into the world, bearing witness to God's reconciling love and plunging ourselves into the struggle against sin, injustice, and violence, a struggle undertaken against overwhelming odds but one in which victory is assured, because in Christ's baptism sin, death, and violence no longer hold sway.

Yet the struggle remains as long as we live. We misunderstand baptism if we think it an assurance that sin, violence, and injustice will disappear in our lifetimes, whether individually or corporately. Calvin recognized this. He continually held out hope for the transformation of society: government was an agent for the common good; Christians were compelled to participate in society toward its betterment; and God's covenant was not simply given for a limited few in the church but established with all creation. His *Institutes*, his masterpiece, concludes with concrete suggestions for how societies might organize themselves to promote the common good and more nearly reflect

God's kingdom. But he was also aware that the full realization of the kingdom would never occur in our lifetimes. Calvin was a hopeful realist, not a utopian. His understanding of baptism, moreover, reflects this hope, as it represents the beginning of a struggle that will never be fully resolved in our lifetimes. Calvin calls this "mortification," the struggle against sin that results in sin's slow death that is never fully accomplished in this life: "We are baptized into the mortification of our flesh, which begins with our baptism and which we pursue day by day and which will, moreover, be accomplished when we pass from this life to the Lord" (4.15.11).

If baptism represents the beginning of a struggle and not its end, how are we to commence in the struggle? Buried within the Larger Catechism of Westminster are some helpful suggestions. Here, the authors of the catechism speak of "improvement in baptism," a theme that has almost disappeared from Reformed vocabulary but one that is essential to maintain in contemporary practice. Without improvement in baptism, we reduce the sacrament to a magical ritual or a mere rite of passage: "The needful but much neglected duty of improving our Baptism is to be performed by us all our life long, especially in the time of temptation, and when we are present at the administration of it to others, by serious and thankful consideration of the nature of it and of the ends for which Christ instituted it . . ." (7.277). The catechism goes on to enumerate "being humbled" by our falling short of grace, "growing up to assurance of pardon of sin," "drawing strength" from Christ's death and resurrection, "endeavoring to live by faith," and walking in "brotherly love." Note how these are not simply things that we do, practices that we muster ourselves into performing. Rather, they are undertaken by grace, given by God in grace, conferred at baptism, and remembered all the days of our life. Baptism gives hope for the transformation of the world (which includes ourselves) not because it changes all things immediately but because it points to the renewal of all things in Jesus Christ. Whenever we baptize others in the church, whenever we remember our baptisms, we, too, participate in the transformation of the world and engage in a struggle that will last until the end of the earth.

QUESTIONS FOR DISCUSSION

1. How is baptism a sign of our hope in God for the future?
2. How do you experience struggle in Christian life? How do you experience growth and improvement in Christian life?
3. How is baptism connected to death? How is it an affirmation of life?

11

The Lord's Supper

ETERNITY AND A MEAL

What is the first thing that comes to mind when you think of eternity? Clouds? Angels? The glory of God? The Danish film *Babette's Feast* offers a vision of eternity that revolves around food. Heaven in this movie comes with a meal. The film depicts a dying Protestant sect that lives communally on a barren stretch of windswept coast. Their life together is marked by strict rules: no unnecessary luxuries; no regard for worldly prestige; much time spent in prayer, worship, and study; and little time for frivolity. They wear simple clothes, eat only enough for sustenance, and don't engage in needless talk. Sound like fun? They don't win many converts. As the film begins, this experiment in communal living is nearing its bitter end. The now elderly members don't seem to like one another anymore. Conversation degenerates into petty bickering, and they don't seem to enjoy themselves or one another. Each one of them is waiting: waiting to die, waiting for the Lord to return, waiting for the last sign of faithfulness to emerge from the group. While they wait, however, the group needs a cook.

Apparently, none of the local Danes are foolish enough to apply for the job. Into their midst wanders Babette, a French immigrant who knows little about the sect's beliefs but needs a job as much as the sect needs a cook. The match is made. At first Babette follows the orders given her: simple food, reasonable portions, given at appointed hours of the day with no excess, frivolity, or anything else that would entice the palate into forbidden pleasures. Day in and day out, the same bland food served in the same silent manner. Then, in an unexpected windfall, Babette receives a large sum of money. Without hesitation, she orders delicacies. Crates of live quail arrive at the sect's door-step, then come cheeses and wines, spices and chocolates. Babette spends excessively and indulgently, breaking all the rules of simplicity that the group has set before her. As she labors to prepare the meal, the members of the sect start grumbling as if to say, What she's doing is blasphemy; she should do something more productive with that money; she's trying to tempt us; maybe she's the devil in disguise. But Babette continues cooking, and at last the meal is prepared. Apprehensive and silent, the aging group sits before strange dishes. No one wants to take the first bite. But then, those gathered around the table begin to taste what Babette has set before them, and to taste this meal is to enjoy. Tastes open their eyes to the beauty of the feast: maybe food is meant not just to fill the belly but also to gladden the heart. As they taste, they start talking. The meal in its hospitality, beauty, and even excessiveness opens them to one another. Members of the group who have ignored each other look each other in the eyes and open to the other's beauty. They begin to talk and even to laugh. The food has become more than food. Wait for eternity? They seem to be experiencing it in a meal cooked by a foreigner who knows little about their ways and less about their religion. Maybe heaven is like that: a place where the hospitality of strangers reigns, where food does not simply fill the belly but opens us to communion with God and one another.

The movie offers, in my reading of it, an extended reflection on Holy Communion, the Lord's Supper. The meal that Babette prepares is a meal *and* more than a meal. The elderly congregation that gathers around this table is fed by the food that Babette prepares but is also fed by the hospitality of the host who gives all that she has. As they eat and drink, moreover, they begin to share with others. Through this meal the embittered believers begin to change as they receive a foretaste of the heavenly banquet. Eternity, in *Babette's Feast*, comes in a meal. For Christians, eternity also comes in a meal, a meal that celebrates the remembrance of the crucified and risen Lord and his promised return.

The book of Isaiah also presents a vision of eternity connected to a meal, in a mountaintop scene that links the end of death with a rich feast:

> On this mountain the Lord of hosts will make for all peoples
>   a feast of rich food, a feast of well-aged wines,
> of rich food filled with marrow, of well-aged wines strained clear.
> And he will destroy on this mountain
>   the shroud that is cast over all peoples,
>   the sheet that is spread over all nations;
> he will swallow up death forever.
> Then the Lord GOD will wipe away the tears from all faces.
>   Isa. 25:6–8a

Isaiah's mountaintop meal is set for everyone, where God's hospitality breaks down the barriers between those who are "in" and those who are "out." Even those whom Israel hates get invited to the banquet, a meal that represents the end of all meals, a meal that nourishes so much that those who taste it will no longer taste death. Eternity, for Isaiah, is something we taste. The Lord's Supper is like that: it offers eternity for the tasting.

Yet the hospitality and abundance of the Lord's Supper contrast markedly with the ways food gets distributed and enjoyed in our globalized society. Ours is a world in which banquets are enjoyed chiefly by the wealthiest while those who supply the food for those banquets struggle to feed their own families. Many of the harvesters of cocoa beans in Cote D'Ivoire, for example, have never tasted chocolate before. This is a world where a very few feast while millions (approximately one in six people worldwide) go hungry every night. The food thrown into dumpsters in North America and Europe could feed millions. In our world people hoard food rather than share it. In our world, the wealthiest who have seats at the table can never get enough delicacies while millions of others do not even have a place under the table to gather up the scraps. The scraps, instead, get wasted and taken to the trash.

In a world that produces enough food to feed its inhabitants, the wealthiest believe in an economy of scarcity in which there is not enough to go around. This world sorely needs the rhythms of the Lord's Table, whose reigning assumption is not scarcity but abundance. This meal does not erect barriers around the feast so that only the most privileged may partake, but assumes there is always more than enough to go around, no matter how many are gathered at Table. Eternity, in Christian faith, comes in a meal, a meal that transforms those who partake of it and the world that celebrates it. Let's look at this meal more closely and what it says about Christian hope for the future and the coming of God's reign.

A MEAL OF REMEMBRANCE

Most of the time, Christians consider the Lord's Supper a meal of remembrance. When we break bread and share the cup together as church, we remember the night on which Jesus was betrayed and how he gave his life for the life of the world. Gathering together, we recall the meal that Jesus hosted with his disciples, a meal that symbolizes his life and death. Remembrance is central to *any* celebration of the Lord's Supper. Without recollection of the events of Jesus' life and ministry, the Supper becomes an ordinary meal.

One of the earliest controversies surrounding the Lord's Supper was that its celebration became somewhat detached from the remembrance of Jesus' death. In 1 Corinthians, Paul indicates that the relative simplicity—even the sober tone—of the meal, as narrated in the Gospels, had become bacchanal and exclusionary: "When you come together, it is not really to eat the Lord's supper. For when the time comes to eat, each of you goes ahead with your own supper, and one goes hungry and another becomes drunk" (1 Cor. 11:20–21). The meal, thus detached from the remembrance of Christ's last meal, had become an example of gluttony and a continuance of patterns that keep food from the hungry. When celebrated rightly, however, the Supper directs us not simply to the food but to the remembrance of Jesus, whose presence is still among us as host. " 'Do this in remembrance of me' " (1 Cor. 11:24b). Every time Christians eat this meal, we remember.

The Reformed tradition has stressed remembrance throughout its history. But what is it that we remember? According to the Second Helvetic Confession, we "keep in fresh remembrance that greatest benefit which he showed to mortal men, namely, that by having given his body and shed his blood he has pardoned all our sins, and redeemed us from eternal death . . . [nourishing] us to eternal life" (5.195). The remembrance, in other words, is of a life that gives life to the world. In recalling the shape of Christ's ministry, in sharing bread and wine, we don't simply remember episodes of a biography that took place in first-century Palestine; rather, we remember these episodes and events as they bring salvation to all.

At Table, we remember the gestures of grace that Jesus embodies. The way that he hosts the meal, the things that he does with his hands are further examples of remembrance. What does Jesus do at the table? In similar strains, Matthew, Mark, and Luke write that Jesus *takes, blesses, breaks, and gives*: "While they were eating, Jesus took a loaf of bread, and after blessing it he broke it, gave it to the disciples, and said, 'Take, eat; this is my body' " (Matt. 26:26). At this meal, we remember that Jesus offers salvation to the world not merely by a sacrificial death, not simply by making satisfaction for the world's sin, and certainly not to appease a God bent on destroying the wicked. Rather, we remember that Jesus saves because of the shape of his life, a life that is taken, blessed, broken, and given.

Jesus takes the bread as he takes his life. Gathering the simple bread set before him, the kind that folks eat every day, Jesus recalls a life that in most instances was quite ordinary: a life that is taken as a gift from God. And in Jesus' gesture of grace, this ordinary loaf of bread becomes his body, just as his ordinary life becomes a revelation of God. All that Jesus is given comes from God; he takes it and directs it back to God.

Jesus blesses the bread and the cup, just as his life is blessed by God, just as his ministry blesses others. Jesus blesses others with his hands, reaching out to tax collectors, lepers, prostitutes, and the bedraggled of society. Jesus touches, blesses, and brings healing to others, lifting up those whom society has beaten down. Salvation, at its root, means healing, and everything that Jesus touches bears witness to healing that can come only from God. Whenever we bless bread at Table, we recall Jesus' touching and blessing of the untouchables.

Jesus breaks the bread and in doing so bears witness to the brokenness of his own body. At the Last Supper, Jesus anticipates the events that will lead to his death on a cross, a form of execution that broke the bones of those who hung in agony. But at this meal Jesus also remembers the brokenness that he *already* bears in his own body: the brokenness of a political regime that could not stomach his witness for the poor and downtrodden; the brokenness of good, religious people who called him a blasphemer. At Table, we, too, bring our brokenness, knowing that Christ has already taken it as his own. His body bears the scars of our brokenness, but his brokenness hardly resembles masochism or the glorification of suffering. Rather, in his brokenness we are healed and fitted for communion. Jesus gives his broken body to the world, just as the bread that he breaks he gives to those who are hungry.

Jesus gives the bread, just as he gives his life. Jesus gives new life not by holding fast to it but by seeing his life in connection with others. Just as the food at the table is not hoarded but is shared, Jesus shares his life with others. In celebrating the Lord's Supper, we remember we gain life not when we clutch it at all costs but when we share it with others. Jesus brings salvation to the world because his is a life given: given by God, given for the world. The church remembers Jesus and the events of his life that bring salvation when it, too, takes, blesses, breaks, and gives bread at Table.

We can learn much about people's lives by paying attention to their last words and actions. If we are aware of our impending deaths, we have time to say our farewells. Jesus says his farewell with a meal, in a gesture of hospitality and thanks, on an occasion of mourning and celebration. His meal invites the disciples to remember him, to recollect what they've learned from him and the time spent with him. But the meal also invites them to *re*-member him, not to simply look backward and recall what Jesus did on their behalf and on behalf of others but to become members of his body by grace, to bear witness in their bodies and their corporate life to the salvation that Jesus brings to the world. At the meal, we bear witness to the belief that broken though we may be, we are also members of one body and in our many gifts we are a response to Jesus' work of salvation. In each of the Gospels Jesus' words at the Last Supper refer very little to past events. Remembering at Table is not the mere recollection of the past, but remembering the promise that the disciples will bear fruit if they abide in him (John 15:1–17).

For Christians gathered around the Lord's Table, there is no golden age to remember. The remembrance of the Supper is not a backward glance that recalls isolated events in the life of a first-century Jewish carpenter. The celebration of Communion in the church, likewise, does not look back to a day when things were good, better, or clearer in the past. Faithfulness to the promises at the Table does not mean the simple repetition of the past. Rather, remembrance, as it re-members, looks to the present and the future as well. Without this forward glance, the church's remembrance becomes a fossil, a shred of its living hope. Christian remembrance at Table also anticipates the reign of God, the coming of Jesus again, and the transformation of the world's hatred and injustice into harmony and peace. Holy Communion is not chiefly a memorial meal; it is an eschatological feast that bears witness to the God who is already coming in Jesus Christ.

A MEAL OF ANTICIPATION

Luke's Gospel records some striking words about the Last Supper. After sharing the cup with his disciples, Jesus tells them, "'For I tell you that from now on I will not drink of the fruit of the vine until the kingdom of God comes'" (Luke 22:18). In giving the cup to his followers, Jesus looks not simply to their present needs and to the promise that he will abide with them even unto death. Rather, his words look forward to the establishment of God's reign, a reign depicted at other places in Luke's Gospel with food and drink. Recall Jesus' earlier words in Luke: "'People will come from east and west, from north and south, and will eat in the kingdom of God'" (13:29). Salvation, for Luke, comes with a meal that is set not for those closest to Jesus but for strangers who come from all corners of the globe. Christians often practice the Lord's Supper as if it were a familiar table set for intimates and friends. We dine with those like us, or at least with those whom we like. But Jesus' forward glance at the Last Supper says something else: He will not drink the cup again until the coming of God's reign, a reign of nuisances and nobodies, strangers and outcasts. The meal that we celebrate, in other words, reminds us that it is important to eat with those whom we *don't like*, for on the day that the kingdom comes, those strangers and enemies become friends.

As the Lord's Supper looks forward to that day, the church celebrates Christ's presence in the church and the world. As we mark that meal with anticipation, we should eat and drink at Christ's Table not occasionally but often. Perhaps the oldest witness to Christian liturgical practice at the Lord's Table comes from 1 Corinthians, where we read, "For as often as you eat this bread and drink this cup, you proclaim the Lord's death until he comes" (1 Cor. 11:26). If proclamation is central to Christian life, then proclamation occurs not simply through our speech, our bearing witness to the crucified

Lord, but in our sharing and consumption of a meal. The sacrament of the Lord's Supper is one place where the words that we speak take flesh. Without the Word, the Supper is only a meal, but without the Supper the Word can become mere talking. Good News takes root in the actions celebrated at Table: giving thanks, breaking, giving, sharing with the world. Christians are by no means seamless practitioners of these gestures, but inasmuch as we celebrate Holy Communion regularly, these practices slowly take shape in our lives, anticipating the kingdom of God where they become permanent.

At Table, Christians look forward not to a utopia—a word that literally means "no place"—but to relationship. The kingdom is witnessed not in the inauguration of some new power that will dethrone all others but in a person, Jesus Christ, who is the end of the violent assertion of power. Christians call the Supper "Holy Communion," a reminder that the meal is always more than the food provided. The meal centers on communion with one another and with the One who makes our relationships with one another possible. In sharing the cup and the loaf, Christians celebrate Christ as the font of communion, recognizing that the healing of relationships comes through him. Whenever we gather at Table, we bear witness to broken relationships, relationships broken by violence on personal and systemic levels, relationships broken by abuses of power so that some have voice while others do not, relationships broken by greed so that some hoard without sharing and live the lie that there is not enough to go around. By sharing at Table, we begin to break down these violent and hoarding patterns, anticipating the healing and wholeness that comes by grace. The Westminster Larger Catechism notes that by receiving the Lord's Supper we confirm our union and communion with Christ (7.278). The church throughout the ages has called this the mystical dimension of Communion, where we become members of the same body with him.

In the church's ordinary practice, we bear witness to how this union is and is not fully accomplished. On the one hand, we are one with Christ. Just as he is the head and we are the members of the body, no life is possible for the members apart from the sustenance we receive from Christ. The union has already been accomplished, and we bear witness to union whenever we partake of Communion. On the other hand, our union with Christ has not yet arrived. Brokenness continues to reign in a world groaning for redemption: beset by state violence that pits ethnic groups against one another; the predatory greed of individuals, corporations and nations; the claims of religion (including Christianity) that breed violence and demonize others. Only a church blind to the injustice and tragedy of the world could glibly proclaim that in Christ we are all one. In celebrating Communion we also bear witness to the hope that God's Spirit will "renew the face of the earth" and that peace and justice will prevail.[1] The union that the Lord's Supper promises is not yet among us, but in celebrating Communion we anticipate its assured emergence on earth.

God's promised healing is always greater than the violence of the world. Yet in a broken world, the contrary often seems the case. Embedded as we are within cycles of violence and suffering, one might think despair is the only option. Christians do not hope because the progress of God's reign is visible for all to see; rather we witness that reign in fits and starts, in partial and imperfect reflections of God's love that emerge in the midst of anguish and horror. One of these places where the hope of God's healing grace appears is at Table. The gestures we follow at Table—taking, blessing, breaking, giving—summon our lives: whether we align ourselves with the relationships and love that sustain and give life or whether we choose the path of violence, greed, and destruction that leads to certain death. When practiced over and again, these gestures become contagious. They do not simply point to Christ's return; they embody hope as they take root in our lives. Rising from the Communion table, we become a people of hope whose lives and actions bear a faint resemblance to the hope given to the world in Jesus Christ, who will surely come again.

As the Confession of 1967 puts it, we rejoice at the Lord's Table in a foretaste of the kingdom, rising to "go out from the Lord's Table with courage and hope for the service" to which Christ has called us (9.52). Here we do not simply receive gifts and wait; here we receive, rise, and go forth. Shaken by the world, we also return to the world as people of hope. (In fact, we've never left it at all, since the Table sits in the middle of the world, celebrating the bounty of the world's harvest.) The command to go forth into the world distinguishes the Lord's Table from a private meal that instills hope for a select few. This Table, by contrast, bears the hope of the world, where all are fed, where swords are beaten into plowshares. At this Table, in the midst of earthly life, we even catch a glimpse of heaven.

A MEAL OF HEAVEN AND EARTH

Christian imagination often places heaven and earth at a vast distance from each other. God is "in heaven" while we are "here below," common wisdom might tell us. Reformed theology consistently stresses that we ought not confuse our desires with God's desires and never substitute something in creation for faith in the one, true God. Indeed, the most notorious abuses in the church have resulted when the church has substituted something else for faith in God. The Reformed tradition calls this substitution *idolatry*. If we are to avoid it, we must never mistake earth for heaven.

Sometimes, however, the impulse to avoid idolatry winds up creating an unbridgeable gulf between heaven and earth. If God is only "in heaven" while we are "here below," we neglect the heart of Christian faith: God makes promises to the world, comes near to the world as the breath of life, and shows this nearness in the flesh of Jesus Christ. The God of Christian faith comes near and brings a taste of heaven to earth. The Eucharist echoes God's nearness. The Heidelberg Catechism communicates the nearness and distance of God witnessed at the Lord's Table: When we eat the body of Christ and drink his blood, we are "to be so united more and more to his blessed body by the Holy Spirit dwelling both in Christ and in us that although he is in heaven and we are on earth, we are nevertheless flesh of his flesh and bone of his bone" (4.076). In this understanding of the Supper, God's nearness is available for the tasting.

Heaven comes to earth in a meal. What I mean by this phrase is not that some remote place, heaven, gets beamed to earth, but that we are united to the God who is other than us in an earthly meal. The Scots Confession claims that the Eucharist bears witness to Christ's two natures—divine and human— so that we might participate in them. At Table, Christ's divinity does not remain remote from us but is given to us in a meal: "As the eternal Godhood has given to the flesh of Christ Jesus, which by nature was corruptible and mortal, life and immortality, so the eating and drinking of the flesh and blood of Christ Jesus does the like for us" (3.21). Christ's divinity, in this view, does not remain separated from us in heaven but transforms us on earth. This is mysticism at its best: heaven comes to earth in a meal.

John Calvin struggled over what it meant to describe Christ's real presence in the Lord's Supper. Unlike the Roman Catholic doctrine of transubstantiation, which points to a change in the substance of the elements themselves (bread and wine are transformed into Christ's body and blood), Calvin's understanding of the Supper points to a change not in the elements but in our reception of them. The bread and wine do not become Christ's body and blood because of priestly words uttered over them. Christ reigns in glory in heaven, and we consume the bread and wine as Christ's body and blood not because he "comes down to us" but because we, by the power of the Holy Spirit, are lifted up to his presence (*Institutes* 4.17.31). The Lord's Supper, for Calvin, is more than an intimation of the messianic banquet, the feasting with Christ in glory. In some way incomprehensible to us, we participate in this banquet and are seated at Table with Christ every time we partake of Holy Communion.

Calvin admits that this understanding of the Supper is difficult to grasp; indeed, we will never truly understand this element of the Supper where the "Spirit truly unites things separated in space" (*Institutes* 4.17.10). The same Christ who reigns in glory is present at Table as we are lifted into his presence. What is miraculous about the Eucharist, for Calvin, is not what it says about the bread and the wine but what it says about us: that by consuming the bread and wine as Christ's body and blood, we are united with Christ in heaven. Reformed Christians have often been accused of having a rationalistic doctrine of the Lord's Supper, a doctrine that keeps the boundaries between heaven and earth fixed and permanent. Some Protestants have thought that bread is really bread and that wine is really wine, and to call them Christ's body and blood is unwarranted sacramentalism. But the language of the union of heaven and earth and of human participation in the divine nature of Christ permeates Reformation-era confessions and Calvin's *Institutes*. In this regard, Reformed Christians can say, along with our Roman Catholic brothers and sisters, that in the Eucharist, "the barrier between earth and heaven has truly been torn open."[2] Heaven comes to earth in a meal.

A MEAL OF ABUNDANCE IN A TIME OF SCARCITY

Christians turn as people of hope to the Lord's Table, where our regular participation in a meal makes us partakers of a heavenly banquet. Yet this participation in divine glory does not mean that we turn a blind eye to all the things that are not heavenly on earth. Ours is a world where the harvested riches of the earth are more often hoarded than shared. Globalization only seems to widen the gulf between rich and poor. While the wealthiest benefit from increasingly intricate webs of global commerce, those who labor in fields and factories, producing the goods and food consumed by the wealthy, are left on the outside looking in. The assumption that governs human behavior in the global North is one of scarcity: There is simply not enough food and wealth to go around; therefore, I'd better hang on to what I've got. This assumption encourages behaviors that, once set, become impossible to break. Why? Because hoarding, like greed, is ultimately insatiable. When I believe that I don't have enough, that there isn't enough to go around, then even when I have more, it still will not be enough. One of the perceptions that unites most Americans is their collective lament that they don't have enough. Regardless of income level, most Americans, when put to the question "What would it take to make you feel like you've really made it?" answer, "Just a little more." Just a little bit more. Then I'll have made it. Then I'll be satisfied. Then I'll be secure. But the reality of American life reveals the contrary. We are never satisfied with what we have, and we think we need just a little bit more. Hence houses continue to increase in size as do our desires for electronic gadgetry and any consumer good that will assure us that we've made it. But those promises and desires are empty. Why? Because scarcity is a lie.

The Lord's Supper operates with different assumptions: not scarcity, but abundance; not hoarding, but sharing.[3] No matter how many gather at the Lord's Table, there is always room for one more. As we share the bread and the wine, all are fed. At Table, we bring the products of our labor, the bread and wine that become the body of Christ as we share them. God takes them, blesses them, and gives us life. To our small response, God gives us God's very self over and over again. Our offering thus becomes God's gift to us. The Eucharistic economy reveals unimagined abundance when things at Table are shared. God gives; we respond in tokens of gratitude; and God keeps on giving, empowering us to give.

In the Eucharistic economy, hoarding leads to death, and sharing, to life. As the medieval mystic Meister Eckhardt once claimed, "There is no such thing as 'my' bread. All bread is ours and given to me, to others through me, and to me through others."[4] Having partaken of this holy meal, sharing in Christ's body and blood, we rise from Table to share this meal and ourselves with the world. It is no coincidence that offerings for the poor accompany celebrations of Holy Communion; without giving and sharing, the meal devolves into gluttony. We come to the Lord's Table hungry, responding to God's work with tokens of our labor in bread and wine; God takes these elements, blesses them, and gives us life, nourishing and satisfying our hungry hearts. Yet we leave the Table not sated but yearning for this food to be shared with all, recognizing that the reign of God is not yet among us, that injustice suppurates in all corners of the globe, that thousands die every day because of hoarded work and hoarded bread. Nourished at the Lord's Table, we also go away hungry, rising from this meal to share ourselves and the bread of our labors.

The Lord's Supper, in other words, is a transformative meal. When work is hoarded, hunger increases as famine; when we are fed at the Lord's Table, our hunger for righteousness and justice grows so that our labor issues forth in bread for the world. We are not simply fed at the meal; we become participants at Table in the work of the kingdom. Union with Christ is not simply something that affects us internally, warming our hearts and sustaining our souls, it transforms our life and work outwardly so that we become participants in Christ's hope for the world. We participate at the Lord's Supper not merely in terms of our consumption but in our extension of the patterns of the Table in life. In a real sense, we only "commune" at Table when the gestures of the Table take root in our lives, when we become sharing and giving people ourselves, hungry for justice, throwing ourselves into the struggles for justice and peace, so that all might have life and have it abundantly. A mixture of hunger and satisfaction, therefore, characterize the Christian celebration of the Lord's Supper. As our thirst is quenched and hunger satisfied every time we eat and drink at the Lord's Table, we hunger that God's reign will come even as we participate in it right now.

QUESTIONS FOR DISCUSSION

1. The Lord's Supper both looks back to the last meal Jesus shared with his disciples and looks forward to the messianic banquet. How do you experience the "backward glance" and the "forward glance" in your life?
2. How does regular celebration of the Lord's Supper affect how we share and celebrate other meals and the gift of food and drink with one another?
3. How do you experience scarcity and abundance in your life?

12

Living Hope

TRUE AND FALSE HOPES

How does the theology explored in this book make a difference in everyday life? Are the themes of resurrection, the Last Judgment, the renewal of heaven and earth, and the kingdom of God simply things that Christians believe about the last days of history? By this point in the book, it should be clear that I am urging Christians to understand the so-called last things not merely as future events but as promises that inform our life here and now. Christians don't simply await the future; they remember the future in Jesus Christ and live into the future by paying close attention to the joy and travail, the suffering and flourishing, of life here and now. The difference that these themes and doctrines make for everyday life is that they encourage Christians to be a people of *hope*: people who are not simply resigned to the present state of affairs but who long and labor for the establishment of God's reign of justice and peace.

"Hope springs eternal." How often have you said these words or heard them in conversation? Most of the times that I have heard them have been in times of perceived hopelessness. The words, in their most typical usage, are meant ironically. Someone may be trying to console a person who has just lost a job, encouraging him that he will find work before long. "Hope springs eternal," the recently unemployed person says, pointing to his disbelief that he will find a job soon. Or someone disillusioned with the current state of political affairs may voice hope in political change. "Hope springs eternal," quips a fellow jaded observer, voicing her belief that real change will never really come, that what counts as change is usually more of the same. The phrase, in its most common use, suggests that hope is irrational, even escapist. Hope blinds our eyes to the misery of the present. It offers us a false comfort that something better lies just down the road, preventing us from seeing the hopelessness right in front of us, staring us in the face.

Is this what hope accomplishes? Is it a false promise of better times tomorrow given in the midst of whatever bogs us down today? Americans, it is often said, are a hopeful people. But many of our hopes fail to deliver on their promises. The so-called American Dream, in its varied forms, often proves elusive. For many, this dream means a rags-to-riches story that is possible for all, making poverty recede like a mirage. If the American Dream proved possible for all, then poverty rates in the United States would decline over time. Yet the inverse has been the case in the last thirty to forty years, particularly among children. American children are more likely to be poor now than at any time in the past thirty-five years. Close to forty percent of children in America now live in low-income families. The promise of material progress, in an American context, often rings false. Even those who live the dream often wind up feeling empty. The promise of higher living standards (once they move beyond lifting people out of poverty) rarely live up to their expectations. The bigger house, the second or third car, and the more exotic getaway rarely lead to increased happiness. More typically, these signs of prosperity simply lead to more stress, increased debt, and an insatiable appetite for more things. Buying into the dream of a higher living standard often leads to cravings that can never be fulfilled. Hope in a better tomorrow based solely on material gain falls flat.

Many American hopes are not so crass. Many of them, in fact, are noble: hope for political leaders to offer courageous leadership during difficult times; hope that ideals of democracy and freedom might spread across the globe. Sometimes we do accomplish great things that gain momentum from our hopes. But at other times we don't. Our hopes for leaders are dashed when we find out they are just as likely to be susceptible to corruption as the previous leader; American ideals get sacrificed upon the altar of realpolitik. The political party or organization that we placed so much hope in winds up catering to the biggest donors rather than the voices of the masses. We often experience, as a people, compromised hope: hopes that hold out much promise and high ideals that eventually cave in to the harsh realities of money and power. Hope springs eternal, but the more things change, the more they stay the same. We may continue to hope, but most of our hopes prove empty in the end. Many of them are false.

One point of this book has been to question this understanding of hope. Hope is not what orients us to an elusive, ever-receding future that promises a brighter day but ultimately fails in its promise. Rather, hope opens our eyes to today, to what God is doing now, as God draws us to the future of God's reign. As a people of hope, we live not blind to the present but embedded within it. Hope is not false but anchors us in what is true, the truth of God's life-giving relation to all that is, witnessed in the life, death, and resurrection of Jesus. Hope orients us not to falsehood and emptiness but to truth. The abiding truth of the cosmos is not the hopes that we project onto the future—the dreams that we paint with our own, often misguided, imagination—but the God who is the embodiment and expression of hope for the world. God is our hope. Living from this hope, the power and presence of God in and among us, revealed to the world in Jesus Christ and sustained by the presence of the Holy Spirit, we live as a people with feet firmly planted on the ground, looking around us, attentive to the cries of injustice and the pain of the present, longing and working for God's reign. Authentic Christian hope does not merely fix our gaze on the future; it turns our attention to the places and people that long for healing, reconciliation, and transformation, grounding our labor for justice and peace in what God has already done. We, as a people of God, attend to past and present as God lures us into the future.

The most significant example of this posture comes in the life of Jesus of Nazareth, an itinerant preacher who proclaimed the imminent coming of God's kingdom. Jesus preached repentance and hope for a kingdom that had not yet arrived. Yet this orientation to the future also turned his attention to the present: healing lepers, sitting at table with the hungry, offering grace in his touch. In Jesus' person, the reign of God has already come, "preaching good news to the poor and release to the captives, teaching by word and deed and blessing the children, healing the sick and binding up the brokenhearted, eating with outcasts, forgiving sinners, and calling all to repent and believe the gospel" (Brief Statement of Faith, 10.2). Jesus breaks bread with those with whom few others would dine; he touches those whom others would rather not touch; he gathers around himself an eclectic mix of people who otherwise shared little in common. He preached the coming kingdom but bore witness to it in his present action. His was a hope that bore fruit in everyday interaction with others. His was a hope that turned attention not merely to an elusive future but to God and neighbor.

BELONGING TO GOD

Christian hope recognizes that we do not belong to ourselves alone; rather, "in life and in death we belong to God," as the Brief Statement of Faith puts it (10.1). Calvin pens this hope another way: "We are not our own. . . . We are God's" (*Institutes* 3.7.1). False hopes encourage us to place trust in things that do not last: good things like political figures, ideologies, family, or cultural identity; or ambiguous things such as money, power, and success. When we place our trust in things other than God, we engage in idolatry. Generally speaking, idols are not bad things that we should dispose of; rather, they are good things that we put in the wrong place. In their proper place, politics, family, culture, and even money enhance the abundance of life. When held as gifts from the Creator, they are meant to be celebrated and nurtured. But when they become the object of our total allegiance, they become problematic. Family cannot in the end represent the fulfillment of life, and when we make it that, family becomes tyrannical and oppressive. The same can be said of politics, culture, and money. They become idols when regarded wrongly, when placed above the Giver of all gifts. All idols, moreover, will decay. But this knowledge often makes us clutch them more firmly in desperation: believing in a political party even when all appearances tell a different story; desperately clinging to a relationship even when it has died. The truth of Christian faith is that we belong not to our idols, but to God. Christian hope liberates us from our idols.

The Reformed tradition has emphasized this difference between hope and idolatry. The point of humanity, as the Westminster Shorter Catechism puts it, is "to glorify God and to enjoy him forever" (7.001). Over and again throughout our history, Reformed Christians have stressed that Christian faith isn't about *us*; it's about *God*. Human life finds fulfillment only as it is oriented toward God. But this chord that we've stressed over the years also has a problematic undercurrent of ignoring human agency and responsibility. Many distortions of the Reformed tradition claim, "Because God has predestined some to salvation, it doesn't really matter in the end what I do in this life"; "Our affairs on earth are mere sandbox play in comparison to God and God's purposes"; "Because God has the 'end' in his hands, all of our efforts to improve things are meaningless"; or, in a somewhat careless citation of John the Baptist, "He must increase, but I must decrease" (John 10:30), implying that I must do less so that God can do more.

The problem with these views of our activity in comparison to God's is that they understand God's action and our action as a zero-sum game. In order for me to "let" God work more fully in my life or in the life of the world, I must "do" less, hang on to less. More God, less me. But is this the way that God really works in life? Is this what we see in the life of Jesus of Nazareth, in Paul, in Moses, in Mary? Does God work more so that we can do less? Or is our agency and God's agency more intricate than that? I would argue the exact opposite: that God animates and sustains our activity, that God's work in the world, in us, does not result in less of ourselves but in an increased sense of our responsibilities as we belong to God. God works in us so that we can become more fully ourselves, creatures responsive to God, responsible for our actions. We see this dynamic consistently in the major figures of the Bible: Moses, Jesus, Paul, and Mary. Moses and Paul do not do less so that God can be revealed more; rather, they understand their activity in the world as the result of an encounter with God; they seek, by grace, to align their labors more fully with God's work of salvation and reconciliation. God, in other words, accomplishes God's purposes in history through the efforts of flawed, inadequate, sinful people, calling them not to give up themselves but to live and work as children of God. Paul, Moses, and even Jesus become the persons they are called by God to be not by giving up on themselves and being passive vessels of divine action but in doing their everyday actions as they grow out of God's grace. Their agency actually increases as God's activity in them increases.

Reformed Christians have often stressed Paul, Moses, and Jesus. With Mary, we've been more ambivalent. Yet the story of annunciation offers another example of God's work in relationship to our activity. When the angel Gabriel visits Mary, telling her that she will give birth to the Son of the Most High, Mary expresses astonishment. After hearing that nothing will be impossible with God, however, Mary says, "'Here am I, the servant of the Lord; let it be with me according to your word'" (Luke 1:38). Mary is more than a vessel for God's activity in this story. She makes haste to visit Elizabeth (Luke 1:39), undergoes the pangs of labor to give birth to the Son, and inquires about her son in the midst of a crowd (Mark 3:31). Mary does not become less of herself so that God can be more. God's work in her increases so that she can be more. Mary, in this sense, contributes to God's work by being who she is. "'Let it be'" is not a sign of passivity; it is a sign of acceptance of who God is and who she is by God's grace. Presbyterian theologian Cynthia Rigby writes, "What leads us to stand in amazement at Mary's participation is that she is both *not* God and essential to God's salvific work."[1] Mary, in this view, can become a model, a figure for all of us: a figure that counters the zero-sum game that we often attribute to God's activity. As persons who belong to God, we are not pawns on a divine chessboard, and we are not people whose work is irrelevant to the coming of God's reign: rather, we become participants in God's reign, by grace, as we become the persons God calls us to be, persons made for relationship with one another and with God. Christian hope stresses nothing less.

LIFE AND DEATH

Death surrounds life. Though we begin our lives without an awareness of death, we soon come to recognize it. Death is built into life: when living

beings run their natural course, they die. But in our age we also understand
death as something that human beings cause, both for themselves and the
earth. The twentieth century was undoubtedly the most brutal of centuries in
terms of war casualties. While more than 100 million people died as a result of
war during the past one hundred years (3,500 people per day), the twenty-first
century does not look much better. Terrorist bombings, preemptive warfare,
and ethnic genocide surround us daily as we surf the Web and watch cable
TV. The more we encounter death, the more we become inured to it. Death
has become so commonplace that it has lost much of its sting, at least when we
watch it on TV or computer screens. Though written before the dawn of the
information age, Howard Thurman's prayer expresses the paralysis that death
often breeds: "We are stifled by the odor of death which envelops our earth,
where in so many places brother fights against brother."[2] As people die in the
streets of American cities and in battlefields across the globe, the planet also
experiences death from human activity: poisoned rivers, fouled air, withering
rain forests, and disappearing topsoil. We seem to be killing ourselves and
other species slowly but surely.

Given these realities, it often appears that death holds the last word. If we
believe that death is the ultimate reality of the cosmos, moreover, that belief
can easily lead to despair, cynicism, and resignation: "It just doesn't matter
what we do, because we're all going to die anyway." Hints of that cynicism
appear in the Bible itself. In the book of Isaiah, the prophet's warning to the
leaders of Jerusalem prompts not repentance in the face of God's judgment
but cynical indifference as citizens prepare for feasting in the face of mount-
ing doom:

> In that day the Lord GOD of hosts
>   called to weeping and mourning,
>   to baldness and putting on sackcloth;
> but instead there was joy and festivity,
>   killing oxen and slaughtering sheep,
>   eating meat and drinking wine.
> "Let us eat and drink,
>   for tomorrow we die."
>   Isa. 22:12–13

In our day, analogous outlooks are common, especially in the wealthiest
nations. We read about melting Antarctic ice shelves over our morning coffee and for a moment are riveted by the urgency of climate change. But this
urgency subsides as we move to another news story that is more lighthearted.
By the time we finish breakfast, we are ready to pile into our car and drive to
work, typically by ourselves, thinking, "There's nothing I can do about climate change. I might as well enjoy the time that I have while I'm here."

Christian faith, however, has a different understanding of death. Christians do not deny the power or reality of death. Resurrection faith does not mean that faithful people no longer need to worry or mourn over death. When a loved one dies, the loss is real and permanent for those who continue to live. Death stings. Reflecting on death, Dietrich Bonhoeffer says that it is nonsense to claim that God fills in the gap that appears when a loved one dies.[3] Resurrection faith is not a cheap comfort that says we no longer need to be concerned with death. Instead, resurrection faith claims that there is a reality in the universe that is stronger than death, and that is life borne of love. We see this most clearly in Jesus' crucifixion and resurrection: out of a horrifying death, a state execution, God brings new life. God raises from the dead the One executed as a criminal. Whatever evil and suffering we face in the world, whatever appalling agony, it cannot squelch hope. The resurrection of Jesus points to God's overcoming of death, a death that God experiences in the Son, and thus experiences in God's very self. What God accomplishes despite Jesus' death, God will also accomplish despite our own death and the death of anything else in creation:

> "Death will be no more;
> mourning and crying and pain will be no more,
> for the first things have passed away."
> Rev. 21:4

Resurrection hope, by remembering what God does in Jesus Christ, anticipates what will happen to all creation in the end of death. Resurrection faith means that love is not only "strong as death, passion fierce as the grave" (Song 8:6), but that God's love and Christ's passion are stronger than death. God's triune love, in other words, is the abiding pulse of the universe.

Unlike a fatalism that resigns itself to the death of the planet, resurrection hope summons us to respond to the life that God gives through acts of healing and reconciliation. In the face of famine among the poor and the hoarding of food by the wealthy, the way of resurrection calls us to share the abundance of earth's harvest. When met with escalating climate change, we do not resign ourselves to its inevitability but work toward concrete measures that lessen the human footprint on the earth. People who live in hope recognize that every day they face a choice, a choice that the covenant people Israel also faced: "I have set before you life and death, blessings and curses. Choose life so that you and your descendants may live" (Deut. 30:19). People who hope seek to discern and sustain life: in places where life is being suffocated, people of hope bear witness to the Holy Spirit—the breath of God—and are animated by the Spirit to work on behalf of life: in health clinics, in disappearing rain forests and emerging community gardens, in advocacy for the poor. It is not up to people of hope to save life, but by witnessing to hope they can sense the emergence of life and work on behalf of life even in the most hopeless circumstances. And because of that witness and work, lives get saved. By laboring for life, many inevitable deaths prove avoidable. In the end, the posture of hope is a wager: there is no proof that life and love are stronger than death. But there is an example and a story, a story of God's faithfulness to a particular people Israel that withstands their unfaithfulness; a story of God's love for the world in Christ stronger than death that a crucifixion could not extinguish. The wager is whether to choose death and to resign oneself to it or to choose life, to labor and give voice to hope all of one's days. Resurrection hope does not mean we wait idly for God; rather, it summons our lives, for the sake of life.

ENDINGS AND BEGINNINGS

Seminary courses in theology commonly discuss the themes of this book during the last week of class. The word *eschatology*, after all, means "doctrine or study of the last things." Often, however, the compressed time of an academic semester causes some introductory courses to run out of time before they discuss these themes. When time runs out, eschatology is typically the first thing to go. As a result, many mainline seminaries and churches tend to avoid the subject of eschatology altogether.

By contrast, end-time scenarios in fundamentalist churches have become increasingly vivid over the past century and a half. The United States has given birth to multiple Christian movements convinced that the end times are upon us. The Left Behind series is only the most recent manifestation of this phenomenon, adding jet fighters, a diabolical secretary general of the UN, and genetic crop engineering to its own interpretation of the last things. In this mind-set, one needs to prepare, because an already scripted end is at hand.

The trajectory of this book has been different from mainline avoidance and apocalyptic expectation. Christian eschatology does not belong at the margins of faith because its concerns are immediate: life and death, resurrection and communion, the kingdom of God and the Last Judgment, baptism and grace. These themes are not appendages to Christian faith; they are integral to its core. Eschatology stands not at the end of Christian faith but is encountered from its beginning. Unlike modern-day apocalypticists, however, I have claimed that eschatology does not focus chiefly on scripted, future events. Eschatology, rather, attends to beginnings as much as endings. If eschatology focuses only on "end things," then Christian faith becomes a strange reflection of ourselves: we meet our Maker; human civilization comes to an end;

and it becomes of paramount importance that we punch our tickets to heaven. Christian eschatology, however, does not center on ourselves but on the God who comes anew every day of life, a hope found on the last pages of the Bible. Instead of announcing the end of all things, the book of Revelation points to new beginnings: "'See, I am making all things new.' . . . 'Surely I am coming soon.' Amen. Come, Lord Jesus!" (Rev. 21:5; 22:20).

Christian hope proclaims the *advent* (coming) of God in Jesus Christ, a hope that begins the liturgical year. At Advent, during a time of anticipation and preparation for the birth of Messiah, the church reads some of the most eschatological texts in the Bible. Here we encounter John the Baptist, proclaiming repentance and the coming of the Day of the Lord. John's hope and expectation pave the way for the Savior's birth. We begin the Christian year by anticipating the Lord's coming, where death will pass away and life will begin anew. In this posture of hope, we both remember and anticipate. Christians remember the death and resurrection of Jesus of Nazareth, and in that remembrance anticipate their own resurrection, creation's renewal, and the world's participation in the glory of God. Christian faith is about new beginnings. Bonhoeffer, as he was led to the gallows in a Nazi concentration camp, embodied this hope when he said his last words: "This is the end—for me the beginning of life."[4] Wherever endings appear decisive, Christians discern in them new beginnings in God's gift of life to the world.

THREE DIMENSIONS OF HOPE

For whom do Christians hope? One of the caricatures of Christian faith is that it's ultimately a selfish matter: Christians believe certain things because these beliefs assure that they inherit eternal life. Christians hope in order to get to heaven. My argument in this book has proceeded along alternative lines. Hope is not chiefly for oneself but for individuals, communities, and the whole of creation.

Individual Dimension. In hoping for the world, Christians hope for themselves as part of this world. The doctrinal foundation of this hope is the resurrection of the body. Each of us, individually and corporately, is made for communion with God. We belong to God in life and death, as the Brief Statement of Faith reminds us. The resurrection of the body instills hope that death does not end our relationship with God, but that God fulfills that relationship in a gift of new life. This individual dimension to hope does not mean that we are destined to live forever: that posture places hope in ourselves all over again and points to an unending passage of time that bears more resemblance to hell than heaven! Rather, the resurrection claims that we are made for relationship with God in and through our bodies. As those who attest to hope in resurrection, moreover, we ought not claim too much about it. We do not know what resurrection looks like. Our biblical and confessional heritage is heavy on metaphor and imagery and short on description. Yet we can claim with confidence that our individuality does not disappear in death, but that it is redeemed and made whole in God's life, encompassing the lives of all bodies. Resurrection faith claims that it is not only our spirit or soul that is made for communion with God but our body as well. The resurrection, moreover, affects not only our hopes for tomorrow but also the way we live today: honoring the body in its grace; nurturing and caring for our body and others'. This individual dimension of hope posits the inestimable worth of every person—male and female, temporarily abled and disabled, young and old, rich and poor. As God blesses and honors the body in the incarnation and resurrection of Jesus Christ, God does not privilege some bodies over others. In Christ, there is no such thing as an ideal body. Each body, in its uniqueness, in God's claim of it, is beautiful. Christians hope for themselves and their bodies because God has taken these bodies as God's own in Jesus Christ, now and forever.

Social Dimension. In hoping for the world, Christians also hope for *others.* Without this social dimension, Christian hope becomes narcissistic. The doctrinal foundation for this hope is the kingdom of God. Jesus proclaimed this kingdom throughout his earthly ministry: in preaching, in healing, in table fellowship. This kingdom tears down barriers that pit persons against one another so that enemies might sit at Table with one another. Christians hope for this kingdom to extend to the whole world, so that swords are beaten into plowshares, so that nation no longer rises up against nation, and peace comes to earth. Christians hope for this kingdom but also practice it when we celebrate Holy Communion, where abundance is shared, where there is always room for one more at Table. When we rise from this Table, its patterns take root in our lives, so that our everyday work and interaction in the world might dimly reflect the abundance of the Host. Christians share food and drink at this Table not chiefly with familiar friends. In practice the Table often becomes a place where like gathers with like. We expect, on Sunday morning, to gather around the Table with people we like. As important as friends are to the social dimension of Christian hope—Jesus, after all, called his disciples friends as he broke bread with them at the Last Supper (John 15:12–17)—we cut short the scope of Christian hope if we restrict the meal to our friends. If friendship is the prerequisite for the meal, then it becomes a cozy dinner club instead of the Lord's Table. We do not set the table and invite others to come; Jesus hosts and invites, even those whom we don't like. Eternity, as Jesus presents it at the Supper, is when those we hate come and share a meal with us, in the process transforming our hatred into friendship.

Because the grace at Table is inexhaustible, the social dimension of Christian hope affects how we live in the world: whether we seek to accumulate or whether we seek to share; whether we lust for power or whether we labor and hunger for justice; whether we accumulate weapons or whether we work for peace. Christians hope for others as the gestures of the Lord's Table suffuse our lives. We do not hope alone.

Cosmic Dimension. In hoping for the world, Christians hope for the renewal of heaven and earth. Christian faith centers neither on the self nor on human society, but on the God who gives life to the *cosmos*. The doctrinal foundation for this hope is the new creation. The God who creates heaven and earth calls creation "good" and intends not their destruction but their renewal in God's very life. Christian hope envisions the communion in the triune life not simply for human persons but for all that is—plants, rocks, stars, blue whales, and comets. God longs for all creation to glorify God. The difference between humanity and the other aspects of God's creation is that everything else—whether a robin, a beetle, a mountain, or a supernova—glorifies God as it is, simply by being itself. We, on the other hand, intend to glorify God but often fail in that endeavor, in self-glorification or self-abnegation.

Christians hope for the renewal of heaven and earth, and this hope translates into concrete acts of care for God's creation. As tenders of the garden, those who hope for the world seek sustainability in agriculture rather than a maximum yield; as stewards of the earth, those who hope recognize that the diminishment of life in any corner of the globe invariably redounds to all who live. As those who long to drink from the water of life, people who hope recognize how precious and imperiled water on this planet is. Hope for the world translates into actions and policies that make our tread on the earth a little lighter. Hope, in Christian imagination, is never idle but reaches out to other creatures and the creation itself.

Christians often have reduced hope to one of these three dimensions. The most common reduction in our era is the individual dimension, as if Christian hope boiled down to life eternal for me. When we do this, however, we reflect our preoccupations with the self and strip the faith of justice, communion, and the wonder of the created world. Yet other oversimplifications of hope have emerged across history. If we emphasize only the social dimension of hope, for example, the nonhuman world evaporates; if we focus only on the cosmic, our individuality disappears and the resurrection of the body recedes from view. It is important, then, to stress all three dimensions as they relate to one another. Christian hope is always more than hope for individuals or society as it embraces all of creation. But hope for creation takes shape only as it pays close attention to the individuals and peoples that populate it. When Christians say, along with the Nicene Creed, that we "believe in one God the Father Almighty, Maker of heaven and earth, and of all things visible and invisible" (1.1), we express our hope for heaven and earth, knowing that all things belong to God.

How, then, do Christians live in light of hope? We are people of hope not when we cling to our lives at all costs but when we hold them lightly, cherishing them as God's gift, laboring for the life of the world. Jesus' claim that "'those who want to save their life will lose it, and those who lose their life for my sake will find it'" (Matt. 16:25) does not mean that we are to surrender our lives and give up on life. Rather, it means that we experience life in its fullness only when we experience it in relation to Jesus' life given for the world. The Christian life is a life of relationship: with others, with creation, with God. Christians bear witness to the hope for communion, the hope that violence and suffering do not have the last word. In the end, which is also the beginning, is the promise of communion and the new life that flourishes because of the communion that is God. That is what we hope for whenever we break bread at Table, whenever we celebrate resurrection, whenever we anticipate the renewal of heaven and earth. Christians hope for the future knowing that the future comes now in Jesus Christ.

QUESTIONS FOR DISCUSSION

1. Do you tend to emphasize one dimension of Christian hope—individual, social, or cosmic—more than the others? Which dimension do you need to emphasize more?
2. Some have said that Christians "remember the future." Do you think this is a helpful way of expressing Christian hope?
3. How does hope turn our attention to today's problems and injustice? How does hope turn our attention away from them?
4. How are Christians to understand death while being people of hope?

Notes

Chapter 2: The Kingdom of God

1. Matthew's preferred phrase for the kingdom is "kingdom of heaven."
2. The phrase is from John Dominic Crossan's *Jesus: A Revolutionary Biography* (San Francisco: HarperCollins, 1994).

Chapter 3: The Resurrection of the Body

1. Aquinas, *Summa Theologica* (Notre Dame, IN: Ave Maria Press, 1981), Supplement q.81, 1.
2. Rudolf Bultmann, *Jesus Christ and Mythology* (New York: Charles Scribner's Sons, 1958), 33.
3. Eugene Rogers, *Sexuality and the Christian Body: Their Way into the Triune God* (Malden, MA: Blackwell Publishers, 1999), 230.
4. I use the word "proven" lightly, since the resurrection, in my view, is not an empirical, historical event that can be proven or disproven through historical investigation or archaeological discovery. It is, rather, a posture of faith, of being claimed and gripped by the truth of the power and source of life in Jesus Christ.

Chapter 4: A Second Coming in Judgment and Grace

1. The phrase is from Shirley Guthrie, *Christian Doctrine*, rev. ed. (Louisville, KY: Westminster John Knox Press, 1994), ch. 19.
2. The South African Truth and Reconciliation Commission, which offered a vision of justice beyond punishment and compensation, presents intriguing and transformative possibilities for justice in societies wracked by racism.
3. Brian Gerrish, ed., *Reformed Theology for the Third Christian Millennium: The 2001 Sprunt Lectures* (Louisville, KY: Westminster John Knox Press, 2003), 7.

Chapter 5: The New Creation

1. Jürgen Moltmann, *God in Creation*, trans. Margaret Kohl (Minneapolis: Fortress Press, 1993), 30.

Chapter 6: What about the Rapture?

1. Charles E. McCoy, "The 'Left Behind' Series: 'Bible Prophecy' or Pure Fiction?" November 18, 2004, http://themilfordchurchofchrist.com/Documents/CEM%20 on%20the%20Left%20Behind%20Series.pdf (accessed April 23, 2010).
2. Tim LaHaye and Jerry B. Jenkins, *Left Behind: A Novel of the Earth's Last Days*, Left Behind (Carol Stream, IL: Tyndale House Publishers, Inc., 1995).
3. Tyndale House Publishers, Inc., "You Don't Need to Be Left Behind," The Official Left Behind Series Site, http://www.leftbehind.com/02_end_times/ end_times.asp (accessed April 23, 2010).
4. The term translated as "coming," *parousia*, was a term in the Greco-Roman world associated with honoring a ruler. The accompanying trumpets are further marks of this imperial honor. Christ, in this sense, is the ruler whom believers honor and welcome as the ruler of all.
5. The image of exorcism is from Amy Plantinga Pauw, "The Holy Spirit and Scripture," in David H. Jensen, ed., *The Lord and Giver of Life: Perspectives on Constructive Pneumatology* (Louisville, KY: Westminster John Knox Press, 2008), 36–39.

Chapter 7: What about Heaven and Hell?

1. Randy Alcorn, "Is Heaven Our Default Destination . . . Or Is Hell?" Eternal Perspective Ministries, http://www.epm.org/artman2/publish/Eternity_Hell/Is_ Heaven_Our_Default_Destination_or_Is_Hell.shtml (accessed April 23, 2010).
2. I will explore this theme more fully in chapter 11.

Chapter 9: What about the Antichrist?

1. Gregory of Nazianzus, "Letters on the Apollinarian Controversy," in Edward R. Hardy, ed., *Christology of the Later Fathers*, LCC (Philadelphia: Westminster Press, 1954), 218.

Chapter 11: The Lord's Supper

1. The phrases are from the Great Thanksgiving of the Eucharistic liturgy found in *The Book of Common Worship* (Louisville, KY: Westminster John Knox Press, 1993), 72.
2. The phrase is from Pope Benedict XVI. See Joseph Cardinal Ratzinger, *God and the World: A Conversation with Peter Seewald*, trans. Henry Taylor (San Francisco: Ignatius Press, 2002), 412.
3. Further reflections on these themes are found in my book *Responsive Labor: A Theology of Work* (Louisville, KY: Westminster John Knox Press, 2006), 67–96.
4. Meister Eckhardt, quoted in Gordon Lathrop, *Holy Ground: A Liturgical Cosmology* (Minneapolis: Fortress Press, 2003), 150.

Chapter 12: Living Hope

1. Cynthia Rigby, "Mary and the Artistry of God," in Beverly Roberts Gaventa and Cynthia L. Rigby, eds. *Blessed One: Protestant Perspectives on Mary* (Louisville, KY: Westminster John Knox Press, 2002),148.
2. Howard Thurman, *Meditations of the Heart* (Boston: Beacon Press, 1981), 187.
3. Dietrich Bonhoeffer, *Letters and Papers from Prison*, ed. Eberhard Bethge, enlarged ed. (New York: Macmillan Publishing Company, 1971), 176.
4. Eberhard Bethge, *Dietrich Bonhoeffer: A Biography*, ed. Victoria J. Barnett, rev. ed. (Minneapolis: Fortress Press, 2000), 927.

For Further Reading

Barth, Karl. "Ending Time." In *Church Dogmatics*, III/2. Edinburgh: T. & T. Clark, 1960.

Calvin, John. *Institutes of the Christian Religion*. Edited by John T. McNeill. Translated by Ford Lewis Battles. 2 vols. Library of Christian Classics. Philadelphia: Westminster Press, 1960. Especially 3.9 and 3.25 ("Meditation on the Future Life" and "The Final Resurrection").

Guthrie, Shirley C. "What's Going to Happen to Us? The Doctrine of the Christian Hope for the Future." In *Christian Doctrine*. Rev. ed. Louisville, KY: Westminster John Knox Press, 1994.

Gutiérrez, Gustavo. "Eschatology and Politics." In *A Theology of Liberation*, 15th anniversary ed. Maryknoll, NY: Orbis Books, 1988.

Hodgson, Peter C. and Robert H. King, eds. "The Kingdom of God and Life Everlasting." Chap. 12 in *Readings in Christian Theology*. Minneapolis: Fortress Press, 1985.

Keller, Catherine. *Apocalypse Now and Then: A Feminist Guide to the End of the World*. Boston: Beacon Press, 1996.

Moltmann, Jürgen. *The Coming of God: Christian Eschatology*. Minneapolis: Fortress Press, 1996.

———. *In the End—the Beginning: The Life of Hope*. Minneapolis: Fortress Press, 2004.

Wilmore, Gayraud S. *Last Things First*. Philadelphia: Westminster Press, 1982.